Conspiracy Beliefs as Coping Behavior

Conspiracy Beliefs as Coping Behavior

Life Stressors, Powerlessness, and Extreme Beliefs

Helen Hendy and Pamela Black

LEXINGTON BOOKS
Lanham • Boulder • New York • London

Published by Lexington Books
An imprint of The Rowman & Littlefield Publishing Group, Inc.
4501 Forbes Boulevard, Suite 200, Lanham, Maryland 20706
www.rowman.com

86-90 Paul Street, London EC2A 4NE

British Library Cataloguing in Publication Information Available

Library of Congress Cataloging-in-Publication Data

Names: Hendy, Helen M., 1950- author. | Black, Pamela, 1955- author.
   Title: Conspiracy beliefs as coping behavior : life stressors,
      powerlessness, and extreme beliefs / Helen M. Hendy and Pamela Black.
   Description: Lanham : Lexington Books, [2022] | Includes bibliographical
      references and index.
   Identifiers: LCCN 2022036880 (print) | LCCN 2022036881 (ebook) | ISBN
      9781666904031 (cloth) | ISBN 9781666904055 (paper) | ISBN
   9781666904048 (epub)
   Subjects: LCSH: Conspiracy theories--Psychological aspects. | Adjustment
      (Psychology) | Belief and doubt.
   Classification: LCC BF773 .H46 2022 (print) | LCC BF773 (ebook) | DDC
      303.3/72--dc23/eng/20220823
   LC record available at https://lccn.loc.gov/2022036880
   LC ebook record available at https://lccn.loc.gov/2022036881

Contents

List of Tables and Figures

Acknowledgments

We are grateful for funding we received from Penn State Hazelton in support of the research described in this book. Additionally, Helen Hendy is appreciative of her most trusted confidants of more than twenty years—Bruce Armstrong, Vicki Johnston, Judy Stephens-Lorenz, Marie Wetzel, and Keith and Sherri Williams. Pamela Black is appreciative of Liz Wright, who has continued to support her research endeavors, no matter how unusual, throughout the years.

Introduction

One story alone dominated the global news markets on January 7, 2021—the violent attack on the US Capitol of January 6, 2021. In France, *Le Monde's* headline was "Trump Provoque le Chaos à Washington," letting Parisians know that President Trump of the United States caused chaos in Washington DC, while *Le Figaro's* readers were informed that democracy was fractured. In Italy, *Corriere Della Sera*'s headline read "Furia di Trump, assalto al Congresso" (Trump's Fury, Assault on Congress), and in Span, *El Pais* proclaimed that "Trump Instiga una Revuelta Contra la Confirmacion de Biden" (Trump Instigates Revolt against Biden Confirmation). Condemnation was not limited to European nations. The *Nigerian Tribune* stated that "Trump supporters defile US democracy." Many of us in the United States, watching it live on our cable news network of choice, noted not only an angry mob, but the symbols of their unity—flags, patches, clothing, colors, accessories—which allowed the rioters to quickly and easily identify other like-minded members of the crowd that day. These symbols included the Proud Boys orange, the Betsy Ross flag that has been co-opted recently by the far-right and antigovernment organizations, the "OK" hand symbol that no longer represents agreement but White power, anything with 1776 on it that allegedly indicates support for a revolution attempting to overturn the results of the 2020 election, the 3 percent sign representing another antigovernment militia group that describes themselves as libertarians, and perhaps most importantly, the letter Q and rabbit symbols that identify followers of the online conspiracy platform QAnon.

The *Oxford English Dictionary* describes conspiracy beliefs as explanations for events pointing to secret plots by powerful others. While the events of January 6, 2021, may lead one to believe that conspiracy beliefs and violent action in support of them are solely the domain of the far right, not only is this not historically the case, but both sides of the political aisle are susceptible to conspiracy theories. Indeed, the bassist for the rather leftist alternative-metal group, Rage Against the Machine, Tim Cummerford, has described himself to *Rolling Stone Magazine* as a conspiracy theorist, stating that he believes the moon landing was a fake, that the terrorist group ISIS is not real, and that the

ISIS beheading videos are a creation of the US government to justify its military action in the Middle East. Nor are left-leaning politicians immune from conspiracy beliefs. Independent Vermont Senator Bernie Sanders has often peppered his political speeches with references to the 1 percent, and while the World Economic Forum has stated that half of the wealth of the world is, indeed, owned by only 1 percent of the population, there does not seem to be any evidence that this group is a cohesive, conspiratorial, and powerful entity.

The purpose of the present book is not to delve into details of conspiracy beliefs from the far right, the far left, or any group in-between. Our goal is to provide new answers to *WHO?* and *WHY?* individuals adopt conspiracy beliefs and willingness to display violence when threatened. More specifically, we examine the *WHO?* of demographic characteristics (such as age, gender, education, income, political affiliation) most associated with a tendency to adopt extreme beliefs. Then, we consider a theory for *WHY?* individuals might adopt extreme beliefs with evaluation of a three-step psychological sequence in which extreme beliefs serve as a "coping mechanism" in response to exposure to life stressors (health, money, loneliness), combined with a sense of powerlessness displayed as post-traumatic stress disorder (PTSD) symptoms such as memory loss, sleep disturbance, hypervigilance, and social withdrawal. This three-step sequence may be summarized as *life stressors → powerlessness as PTSD → extreme beliefs.*

In part 1, we review theoretical perspectives on conspiracy ideation, as well as past research on demographic and psychological variables found associated with adoption of extreme beliefs. Some theories we include offer understanding of conspiracy ideation at a macro or sociological level (such as resource competition, or the role of structural uncertainty), while other theories offer understanding at a more micro or psychological level, which will guide our book's evaluation of psychologically *WHY?* individuals adopt extreme beliefs. More specifically, we will use principles of the threat appraisal and coping theory (Lazarus and Folkman, 1984) to propose that adoption of extreme beliefs may serve as a "cognitive coping mechanism" when individuals experience severe life stressors (health, money, social) combined with a sense of powerlessness (displayed as PTSD symptoms), perhaps because these extreme beliefs offer them a sense of understanding, strength, and community with other like-minded individuals.

In part 2, we discuss specific conspiracy theories in an historical context. They have been around since at least the time of the Roman Empire, and they have thrived ever since. We focus on conspiracy beliefs found mostly in the United States, but with mention of other more international beliefs. We consider the events of September 11, 2001, as our cut-off point for historical conspiracy theories, with the view that conspiracy theories since 9/11 are contemporary because there is still widespread support for them. Granted, conspiracy theories about the moon landing or the Kennedy assassination are still around, but support for them seems to have paled in comparison with more recent ones. We do include UFO sightings and alien conspiracy theories as contemporary beliefs, especially since the sightings from June 21, 2021, above Las Vegas and the rather ambiguous government statements about them seem to have stirred renewed interest in all things UFO. However, our review of historical and contemporary conspiracy beliefs does *not* include coverage of localized religious cults that follow a charismatic leader (such as Jonestown and Heaven's Gate) even though their indoctrination may incorporate some of the conspiracy beliefs we review. Finally, in part 2 we specify the purpose of the present study and its hypotheses for a sequence of psychological variables we believe lead to increased risk for conspiracy beliefs and violent ideation: *life stressors* → *powerlessness as PTSD* → *extreme beliefs*.

In part 3, we describe the research methodology (participants, procedures, measurement of variables) that we use to examine demographic characteristics (*WHO?*) and psychological characteristics (*WHY?*) associated with five general types of conspiracy beliefs for a nationwide sample of US adults. Demographics we consider include age, gender, racial identity, ethnic identity, college education, employment, income, partner status, household size, social media exposure, military experience, regional environment, and political affiliation. Psychological characteristics we consider include three perceived life stressors (health, money, loneliness), and displayed powerlessness in the form of post-traumatic stress disorder (PTSD) symptoms. Our outcome measures of extreme beliefs include five general types of conspiracy beliefs (government malfeasance, malevolent world power, extraterrestrial coverup, personal well-being threat, control of information) as identified by Brotherton, French, and Pickering (2013), as well as violent ideation, or the person's willingness to display violence when threatened.

In part 4, we describe the statistical analyses we use to examine first the *WHO?* of extreme beliefs as identification of demographic characteristics most associated with extreme beliefs (the five conspiracy theories and violent ideation). Then we examine our proposed *WHY?* of extreme beliefs as a three-step psychological sequence in which life stressors, combined with PTSD powerlessness, are associated with increased risk for extreme beliefs: *life stressors* → *powerlessness as PTSD* → *extreme beliefs*. In this section, we also include tables and figures to show in great detail the findings from our nationwide sample of US adults.

In part 5, we summarize our study results and make interpretations for how well they match the patterns of variable relationships that we hypothesized. Based on our findings, we also offer suggestions of intervention approaches for those (counselors, parents, individuals themselves) who might wish to reduce the risk of extreme beliefs concerning conspiracies and violence. Finally, we describe limitations of the present study and give recommendations for future research on extreme beliefs.

PART 1

Theoretical Perspectives on Conspiracy Beliefs

Chapter 1

Theoretical Perspectives on Conspiracy Beliefs

Prior to the presentation of our research on *WHO?* tends to adopt extreme beliefs and psychologically *WHY?* they may do so, it is necessary to sketch out theoretical frameworks that guided our hypotheses for demographic and psychological variables associated with conspiracy beliefs and violent ideation. As authors, our professional backgrounds are as a sociologist and a psychologist, so in this chapter we describe theories from our respective disciplines that we believe suggest predictors of extreme beliefs, first from a more macro or sociological perspective, and then from a more micro or psychological perspective. These theories from our disciplines both emphasize the importance of two variables for understanding triggers for extreme behaviors: intense life stressors/strains, combined with a sense of powerlessness.

SOCIOLOGICAL THEORY

Anomie or Strain

The general concept behind anomie or strain theories is that humans are often faced with stressors in their lives that prompt them to cope with positive strategies or more deviant strategies to restore a sense of balance to their lives. Conspiracy ideation, especially in the case of some of the more extreme conspiracies, may be considered a deviant belief system, and it may help individuals cope with life strains by creating a sense of community or belonging where none other exists.

Emile Durkheim (1897) found that especially in societies characterized by individualism, social norms or expectations for behavior can breakdown and blur, which tends to reduce society's ability to regulate its citizens' conduct. This dysregulation of behavior tends to be especially pronounced during times of rapid social change, which may explain why conspiracies become more popular when society is in turmoil, such as with the recent US presidential election drama and the global COVID-19 pandemic.

Robert Merton (1968) expanded Durkheim's concept of anomie to describe the disjunction that may occur between the goals society proposes for its citizens, while not always providing the means for them to achieve those goals. For example, the view that in America anyone can succeed if they try hard enough is often incompatible with the reality that not everyone has equal access to the resources needed to succeed (such as safe housing, education, employment, health care). Merton specifically noted that individuals from the lower socioeconomic classes of society may be most likely to feel this strain, which could perhaps explain a greater appeal of conspiracy theories for individuals who feel that American society has moved on and left them behind, forgotten.

General strain theory (or GST) was developed by Robert Agnew in 1992, proposing that individuals whose limited access to resources places them at a less advantaged position in society may be at increased risk for deciding to engage in behavior considered deviant by that society. People who strongly support conspiracy theories may do so because they do not have adequate resources to deal more constructively with the poverty, frustration, and/or loneliness they feel in their own lives. For example, perhaps the frustration among some of the January 6 Oath Keepers that "your champion is no longer in office" prompted them to rationalize this loss by believing that the election was stolen. It may also have given them a community of like-minded individuals that helped them rebuild a strong sense of social identity.

Social Identity

Social identity theory states that an individual's sense of self is based on their group membership. Tajfel (1974) proposed that the groups to which we belong (such as family, football fans, political party) give us not only a sense of pride and enhanced self-esteem, but also social identity or a marker of where we belong in society. A few years later, Turner, Brown and Tajfel (1979) identified the three stages of social identity: categorization, identification, and comparison. Social identity theory and its processes can be nicely illustrated by the conspiracies (and subsequent behavior) surrounding the COVID-19 mitigation mandates of 2020 to 2022.

The first step in social identity formation is categorization. This process requires one to simply take a look around and see what groups are out there. At the start of the pandemic, with many of us quarantined at home, or taking our chances with the virus out in public, it was easy to identify the different groups. Anti-maskers (or later, anti-vaccine groups) were easy to identify. Clearly, those not wearing masks were part of one identifiable group, and those wearing masks everywhere were part of another identifiable group (taking into account that, for illustration, we are dichotomizing people here as either pro-mask or anti-mask). Social media played its part to enhance the divide between these social identities, being filled with posts such as "it is my choice to not wear a mask" or "wearing a mask is the socially responsible thing to do."

The second step in social identity formation is identification. Once we have identified the possible groups in society, we must decide to which group we belong. Scrolling through Facebook, or Instagram, or Snapchat, we can get a pretty good sense of who thinks like us, and who definitely does not. During the pandemic, isolated at home, we could also share memes or videos or news stories that support our growing point of view. The more "likes" and "shares" we get, the more we feel recognized, important, and belonging with these other people.

The final step in social identity formation is comparison. We tend to increasingly compare ourselves and our group to "the others." Again, the COVID-19 pandemic illustrates this process beautifully. Imagine you are pro-mask, even now, years into the pandemic. You have your Facebook friends and your Instagram followers who are also pro-mask. You share news stories, CDC reports about the new variant, outrageous memes and videos about anti-maskers, such as the story about the dad in Texas who stripped down at a school board meeting to make a point about not wearing clothing he dislikes for the good of society (Teh, 2021). Every shared story and every "like" it receives further cements your membership in the pro-mask group, making you feel you belong with them. Your neighbor, vehemently anti-mask, does the same, this time targeting the mask-wearing crowd. Every time they walk into Walmart without a mask or keep their child home from school to protest mask mandates, they get more "likes" and more "social capital" on social media. For both you and your neighbor, "the enemy" has now been identified, and it strengthens your ties to your group. Similarly, sharing conspiracy beliefs on social media can grease the wheels of in-group membership.

Powerlessness

As described by Hammell (2006), people feel powerless when they do not have decision-making power. She notes that this is particularly likely when the chasm is wide between those with resources and power in society, and those without these advantages. Hiroto and Seligman (1975) extended to human behavior the findings of earlier studies of the paralyzing effect on animals when faced with painful conditions, but "helpless" to change them. Their concept of "learned helplessness" posits that when people believe they are unable to exert control over negative environments their lives, they may cease trying to change these conditions, develop anxiety and depression symptoms or, as we believe, adopt conspiracy beliefs and participate in communities of similar believers to regain a sense of power or control. For example, some prepandemic research suggests that group membership identification can lead to perceptions of increase power (Moon, 2013). Therefore, it is easy to see the attraction of "stolen election" or "COVID hoax" conspiracies for individuals who believe that they are disadvantaged in access to resources, disenfranchised politically, and helpless to change conditions that matter to them. By identifying with individuals who hold similar conspiracy beliefs, they may at least temporarily improve perceptions of their insight, power, and community.

PSYCHOLOGICAL THEORY

Similar to the sociological concepts of strain, perceived powerlessness, and a resulting need for social identity to ease their distress, the psychological concepts of the threat appraisal and coping theory (Lazarus and Folkman, 1984) propose that when individuals experience life stressors (such as from health, money, or social challenges), especially when combined with a sense of powerless in the face of these stressors, they become motivated to use various coping behaviors to relieve their distress and to feel more powerful. These coping behaviors may include adaptive actions that give both immediate distraction as well as strengthening them against future stressors. Examples of such adaptive coping behaviors for individuals in a variety of circumstances may include social support, exercise, quality sleep, altruism, faith, creative expression, and exposure to nature (Amadi, Uwakwe, Odinka, Ndukuba, Muomah, & Ohaeri, 2015; Berger & Tiry, 2012; Bergland, Thorsen, & Loland, 2010; Budge, Adelson, & Howard, 2013; Chen & Feeley, 2014; Cox, Owen, & Ogrodniczuk, 2017; Hartley, Fleay, & Tye, 2017, Jackson, 2013, Lee, Joo, & Choi, 2013; Matthews, Hall, Cousins, & Lee, 2016; Norris & Mitchell, 2014; Shishehgar, Mahmoodi, Dolatian, Mahmoodi, Bakhtiary, & Alavi Majd, 2013; Smith, Hancock, Blake-Mortimer, & Eckert, 2007; Tada, 2017; Theadom, Cropley, & Humphrey, 2007; Ulrich-Lai, Christiansen, Ostrander, Jones, Jones, Choi, & McEwen, 2010; Wiborg, Knoop, Stutemeijer, Prins, & Bleijenberg, 2010).

However, some coping behaviors may be more maladaptive actions that offer immediate distraction and a sense of being powerful, but at the cost of later negative consequences such as physical harm, addiction, or arrest. Examples of such maladaptive coping behaviors may include substance abuse, spending sprees, violence, and perhaps adoption of extreme beliefs.

More specifically, principles of the threat appraisal and coping theory would suggest the following variable sequence as one way to understand the pathway toward extreme beliefs: *life stressors → powerlessness as PTSD → extreme beliefs*. Support for this three-variable sequence between life stressors and maladaptive coping behaviors has been found for variety of deviant behaviors including hoarding, disordered eating, medication misuse, opioid addiction, and violence (Black, 2018; Black & Hendy, 2018; Camlibel, Can, & Hendy, 2021; Hendy, Black, Can, Fleischut, & Aksen, 2018). Coping behaviors that allow the release of *anger* or violence may be especially appealing to individuals experiencing stressors and powerlessness because, uniquely for strong emotions (sadness, fear, disgust, happiness, surprise), anger tends to make individuals feel more energized, powerful, and blameless (Herrero, Gadea, Rodriguez-Alarcon, Espert, & Salvador, 2010; Kazén, Kuenne, Frankenberg, & Quirin, 2012).

CONCLUSION

As authors of the present book, we have offered sociological and psychological theories from our respective disciplines that we believe may help to explain increased risk for extreme beliefs such as conspiracies and violence. What the above theories have in common is that they all propose a sequence in which individuals who face intense *life stressors* (health, money, loneliness), and who experience symptoms of *powerlessness*, become at increased risk for adoption of *extreme beliefs* as cognitive coping mechanisms that might restore their sense of power and community. In the next chapter we review some of the most current research on demographic characteristics associated with conspiracy beliefs (in preliminary answer to the question of *WHO?* adopts them), and on psychological characteristics associated with conspiracy beliefs (in preliminary answer to the question of *WHY?* they adopt them).

Chapter 2

Past Research on *WHO?* and Psychologically *WHY?* People Adopt Conspiracy Beliefs

This chapter discusses the relatively limited past research on demographic characteristics (*WHO?*) and psychological characteristics (*WHY?*) associated with adoption of extreme beliefs. While the general perception may be that in the United States it is older, White, poorly educated males with loneliness or poor mental health who are the biggest consumers of conspiracy theories, past literature sometimes suggests otherwise. For example, as described below, existing research is contradictory concerning how gender and age are associated with conspiracy beliefs. However, as expected from the above stereotype, past research has found that individuals with lower socioeconomic status (poor education plus poor income) are more likely to adopt conspiracy beliefs. Then again, unlike the stereotype that White individuals are most likely to adopt conspiracy beliefs, available research suggests that ethnic minorities may be more likely to do so, particularly in conspiracy theories of governmental malfeasance. Given the history of government mistreatment of ethnic minorities (such as the infamous Tuskegee experiment in which Black men were intentionally given syphilis to document its progression), perhaps this finding is not so surprising after all.

As described below, existing research on psychological factors linked with conspiracy beliefs is perhaps more as expected from the above stereotype. For example, psychotic disorders and, to a lesser extent, depression and anxiety have been found associated with increased risk for extreme beliefs. Also, past research supports the idea that isolated individuals or those with a sense of powerlessness are more likely to adopt conspiracy theories. Perhaps sharing their extreme beliefs with interested others facilitates perceptions of strength and belonging to a community, giving them a "social identity" and clarifying for them who is in the in-group and who is in the out-group.

WHO?—DEMOGRAPHIC CHARACTERISTICS
ASSOCIATED WITH CONSPIRACY BELIEFS

Gender

Some research has found that females were more likely than males to believe in conspiracy theories (Abraham, Adorjan, Ahmed, Auwal, Bjedov, Bobes, et al., 2022). Other research (Dyrendal, Kennair, & Bendixen, 2021) found few gender differences in conspiracy ideation, except that women were more likely to hold paranormal beliefs. In a study specifically focusing on COVID-19 conspiracies, Natoli and Marques (2021) found that gender did not moderate the relationship between conspiracy beliefs and intention to practice COVID-mitigation policies. Prichard and Christman (2020), focusing solely on the conspiracy belief that China was intentionally responsible for the creation of the COVID-19 virus, found that men were less worried about the virus than were women.

Age

There exists a stereotype of the conspiracy theorist as the socially isolated baby boomer, glued to the computer screen, searching for theories to support their beliefs about the world. However, a recent study (Buturoiu, Udrea, Oprea, & Corbu, 2021) did not find any evidence that age plays a role in conspiracy theory beliefs about the COVID-19 pandemic, but they do acknowledge that other prepandemic studies have found older people to be more prone to believing conspiracy theories. In contrast, Radnitz and Underwood (2017) and Swami (2012) found that it was younger people who were more likely to accept conspiracy theories, particularly when feeling politically powerless (Romer & Jamieson, 2020), although this may be associated with increased social media consumption by these younger adults.

Education and Income

Education and income are traditionally indicators of socioeconomic status. Past research has found education to be negatively associated with belief in conspiracy theories (Carey, 2019; van Prooijen, 2016). One interpretation of these patterns would be that education provides individuals with more possible explanations for life's most confusing and stressful events, which improves their sense of power or efficacy. While not directly linking income to conspiracy ideation, Andrade (2021) found that marginalized ethnic groups in Venezuela, who were generally less financially well-off, were more likely to believe conspiracy theories.

Race and Ethnicity

As previously noted, Andrade (2021) found that ethnic minority college students in Venezuela were more likely to believe in conspiracy theories. Davis, Wetherell, and Henry (2018) noted that Black Americans were more likely than White Americans to support conspiracy theories, especially those related to systemic racism. In a study of vaccine hesitancy in the United States, another study (Stroope, Kroeger, Williams, & Baker, 2021) also found that Blacks and Hispanics were also most likely to believe in governmental conspiracies, with Blacks more likely than Whites to support theories of governmental conspiracies against Blacks (Crocker, Luhtanen, Broadnax, & Blaine, 1999). Similarly, another early study (Klonoff & Landrine, 1999) revealed that about 25 percent of Black study participants believed that the HIV/AIDS was a virus created by the government to kill Blacks.

WHY?—PSYCHOLOGICAL CHARACTERISTICS ASSOCIATED WITH CONSPIRACY BELIEFS

Mental Health

Some research suggests that individuals high in anxiety or perceived helplessness may be at increased risk for adopting conspiracy beliefs (Abalakina-Paap, Stephan, Craig, & Gregory, 1999; Green & Douglas, 2018; Grzesiak-Feldman, 2013; Newheiser, Farias, & Tausch, 2011; Pratt, 2003; Radnitz & Underwood, 2017; Swami, Furnham, Smyth, Weis, Lay, & Clow, 2016; Zarefsky, 2014). In addition, Barron and colleagues (2014) found that people high on the schizotypy spectrum may give more credence to conspiracy theories. Schizotypal persons fall along a continuum, ranging from very mild to a diagnosis of schizophrenia, characterized by a near complete rejection of reality. They are often creative, artistic, impulsive, and superstitious. The Mayo Clinic (https://www.mayoclinic.org/diseases-conditions/schizotypal-personality-disorder/symptoms-causes/syc-20353919) also describes people with this type of personality disorder as being eccentric, without close relationships, and with trouble understanding how their behavior affects others. They tend to be distrustful, misinterpret the behavior and motives of other people in a negative way, and adopt unusual beliefs or delusions, all of which increase their risk for conspiracy ideation.

Prior to the COVID-19 pandemic, researchers explored how two versions of anxiety were associated with conspiracy ideation (Grzesiak-Feldman, 2013), finding that trait anxiety (pervasive perceptions of stress, worry, or discomfort) tends to increase the probability of conspiracy beliefs concerning ethnicity or nationality, whereas state anxiety (temporary distress as a reaction to events) does not. Additionally, individuals with anxious-attachment style (insecurity in personal relationships) may be at increased risk for belief in conspiracies (Green & Douglas, 2018). Finally, when Abraham and colleagues (2022) dichotomized mental health problems into psychotic or reality-distorting disorders (such as schizophrenia, bipolar disorder) and nonpsychotic disorders (such as anxiety and depression), they found that individuals with psychotic disorders were more likely to believe in conspiracy theories than were those with nonpsychotic disorders.

Of course, the COVID-19 global pandemic spurred not only an increase in conspiracy theories, but also interest in studying people who adopt these beliefs. Research published early in the pandemic (Šrol, Mikušková, & Čavojová, 2020) found that lack of institutional trust during the early days of the pandemic was related to increased anxiety and perceptions of powerlessness, but that only the perception of powerlessness was associated with COVID-related conspiracy beliefs. In an interesting twist that demonstrates the challenge of untangling the *cause-effect* direction of these associations, some researchers (Leibovitz, Shamblaw, Rumas, & Best, 2021; Simione, Vagni, Gnagnarella, Bersani, & Pajardi, 2021) have "flipped the script," proposing that conspiracy ideation is involved in the *creation* of anxiety. In any case, in their recent review of the literature on psychological factors associated with conspiracy ideation, Goreis and Voracek (2019) note the need for stronger theoretical interpretations for how psychological factors combine to increase the risk for conspiracy beliefs.

Social Isolation or Loneliness

Individuals who experience *anomie*, or the sense of social isolation and mistrust of other people, may be more inclined to believe conspiracy theories, although *correlations* between these variables are not evidence of the direction of *causal* relationships. For example, it could be that isolation prompts individuals to adopt explanations for why people treat them badly, or it could be that adoption of these beliefs prompts them to avoid people who may be part of the *plot*. Similarly, other researchers (Douglas, Uscinski, Sutton, Cichocka, Nefes, Ang, & Deravi, 2019; Hettich, Beutel, Ernst, Schliessler, Kampling, Kruse & Braehler, 2022; Marques, Ling, Williams, Kerr, & McLennan, 2022; McCarthy, Murphy, Sargeant, & Williamson, 2021; Poon, Chen, & Wong, 2020) suggests that individuals who were more socially isolated were also more likely to support various conspiracy theories such as those about politics, the pandemic, and extraterrestrials. To no one's surprise, the lockdown conditions required during the early COVID pandemic exacerbated feelings of isolation, driving many US citizens to online social groups, with some of these remote communities reinforcing acceptance and propagation of conspiracy theories (Dow, Johnson, Wang, Whitson, & Menon, 2021).

Social Identity

But why would anomie or loneliness make conspiracy theories more appealing? Social identity theory may explain the attractiveness of conspiracy theory beliefs as a way for isolated individuals to feel more as if they have social identity and "belong" to a group. In this book, we are suggesting that belief in conspiracy theories can serve as a glue or lubrication that facilitates ingroup relationships. For example, individuals with strong *political affiliation* may find conspiracy theories particularly attractive because they provide a *shared* view of the world that unites them with other like-minded people (Tymoshenko, 2017), and learning that an idea is considered a "conspiracy theory" does not reduce belief in it (Wood, 2016). Although strong political identity of either liberal or conservative leanings may increase such attraction to conspiracy beliefs, this effect may depend upon the prevailing political climate and which political party is in power. For example, the present US nationwide survey was conducted during the COVID-19 pandemic and while Democrats controlled the presidency, the Senate, and the House of Representatives, so we anticipated that study participants with *conservative* leanings would be more likely to embrace conspiracy beliefs for the sense of empowerment and bonding they offered.

Most of the past research that has examined associations between social identity and conspiracy beliefs was conducted prepandemic. For example, Sapountzis and Condor (2013) studied Greek citizens at the time of the "Macedonian crisis" in which Greece declined to recognize the name Macedonia, prompting much controversy within the European Union (EU) and NATO. These researchers concluded that "conspiratorial reasoning" served as a form of "intergroup representation" that strengthened in-group and out-group identification. Similarly, a study in Indonesia (Mashuri & Zaduqisti, 2015) found that when their participants reported a strong "Muslim identity," they held stronger conspiracy beliefs. Also, Anthony and Moulding (2020) noted, as we hypothesize, that political identity influenced their participants' beliefs in the conspiracy of "fake news" to manipulate people by controlling their information. More recently, studies have found strong associations between conspiracy beliefs and the person's agreement with "national narcissism," or the view that their own nation is the center of the world and entitled to special treatment (Cookson, Jolley, Dempsey, & Povey, 2021; Sternisko, Cichocka, Cislak, & Van Bavel, 2021; van Prooijen & Song, 2020).

Powerlessness

Why is belonging to a group so important to people, and how can it increase their sense of power in the face of life stressors? Uscinski and Parent (2014) suggest that widening power differentials are the primary drivers behind conspiracy theories, and the available research supports this idea. Humans are social beings, and there is a saying that "strength lies in numbers." As with many other social animals, we tend to feel safer and stronger when we are part of a group, and people may turn to conspiracy beliefs when they experience life stressors and experience a sense of powerlessness (Abalakina-Paap et al., 1999; Pratt, 2003; Zarefsky, 2014). Most of the research on associations between powerlessness and conspiracy beliefs has been conducted after the COVID-19 pandemic shut down the world in March of 2020. However, a study in 1999 (Crocker et al., 1999) found that Black college students were more likely than White students to believe in the existence of "systemic racism," or a conspiracy by the US government to target Black Americans. Also, the stronger the Black students' belief in systemic racism, the higher their racial self-esteem, which could represent that sense of empowerment and bonding available when individuals identify themselves as part of a group, even an oppressed group. Once again to show that the *cause-effect* direction of correlations is always open to interpretation, Jolley and Douglas (2013) concluded that conspiracy theory ideation *reduced* their study participants' inclination to be engaged politically, especially when they had perceived powerlessness. Another challenge to researchers is the measurement of such "powerlessness." One approach would be to ask study participants their *perceptions* of powerlessness, or poor "internal locus of control" (Lao, 1978; Levenson, 1972). However, it may be that even when individuals believe they have complete control over their life stressors, they may be *displaying* powerlessness in many areas of their life that resemble the symptoms of post-traumatic stress disorder (PTSD) with its problems of distractibility, poor memory, insomnia, nightmares, hyper-reactivity, irritability, and social withdrawal (Foa, Cashman, Jaycox, & Perry, 1997).

With the COVID-related conspiracy beliefs that emerged as the pandemic raged (such as that it was created in the lab intentionally by China, that the US government would use vaccination to insert tracking devices into its citizens), researchers turned their attention to them, often finding that powerlessness was an important variable in relationships between political leanings and conspiracy beliefs. For example, a study in Croatia (Tonković, Dumančić, Jelić, & Čorkalo Biruški, 2021) found that their participants' sense of political powerlessness was a strong predictor of COVID-related conspiracies. Another study (Biddlestone, Green, & Douglas, 2020) found that individuals with strong "horizontal collectivism" (for the good of the community) world views at reduced risk for perceiving powerlessness, and more likely to adhere to government recommended COVID mitigation measures such as with social distancing and wearing masks, presumably dismissing COVID-related conspiracy beliefs. In contrast, individuals with strong "vertical individualism" (for the good of the individual) world views were more likely to experience a sense of powerlessness, and they were more likely to adopt conspiracy beliefs concerning COVID. Other researchers have found links between feelings of powerlessness, belief in COVID-related conspiracies, and reluctance to get vaccinated for COVID (Lo, Li, & Wu, 2021).

CONCLUSION

In summary, it appears from past research that a preliminary answer to *WHO?* adopts conspiracy theories may be that these extreme beliefs are more common for individuals with younger age, female gender, Black racial identity, less college education, and conservative political affiliation. Additionally, it appears from past research that a preliminary answer to psychologically WHY? people adopt conspiracy theories may be that these individuals often experience anxiety, loneliness, and a sense of powerlessness, so adoption of these extreme beliefs may in some way offer them relief from their stressors. Part 2 of this book describes examples of conspiracy theories across the centuries that may have served this function for their believers.

PART 2

Conspiracy Theories in a Historical Context

Chapter 3

Conspiracy Theories in a Historical Context

While conspiracy theories have no doubt gained a fair amount of public attention in recent years, they are by no means a new phenomenon or unique to our era of social media overconsumption. While many of the earliest recorded conspiracy theories focused primarily on political figures, technical advances in communication have probably expanded them to other human concerns. One consistent pattern that does emerge across the ages, however, is that conspiracy theories tend to crop up during times of major political and social upheaval. For example, as described below, theories surrounded the death of Roman Emperor Nero occurred during the rise of Christianity. Also, conspiracy theories surrounding the Freemasons and the Illuminati originated during the Renaissance and the Enlightenment, a period in which Europe saw unprecedented social change, world exploration, and scientific discoveries. Additionally, the gradual decline of the Cold War between the United States and the Soviet Union saw conspiracy theories described below concerning the death of President Kennedy, the moon landing, the secret New World Order, extraterrestrial coverup, and fear of FEMA concentration camps. While the 1990s may seem relatively tame compared to other decades, doomsday preppers developed mistrust in the government and technology as the new millennium approached. During the past twenty years, the explosion of the internet and social media platforms has allowed conspiracy theories to proliferate wildly in response to any new or puzzling phenomenon. In this chapter, we review early conspiracy theories in the 2000 years leading up to the new millennium of the twenty-first century. Then in the next chapter, we review some of the most contemporary conspiracy beliefs.

EARLY CONSPIRACY THEORIES

Nero (68 AD)

One of the earliest recorded conspiracy theory surrounds the death of the Roman Emperor Nero, who committed suicide at age thirty in 68 AD. Relatively unpopular and facing a revolt, he had his secretary kill him (Bunson, 2009). Suspicion surrounded his death, or possibly his nondeath, and Rome descended into chaos while politics played themselves out (Schaff & Wace, 1890).

Some contemporary conspiracy theories posited that Nero had, in fact, faked his death in order to outwit his rivals (Blount, 2009), hiding in the eastern part of the empire, biding his time. Some, particularly Christians, believed that he was dead, but that, like Jesus Christ, he would rise from the dead and regain his throne (Blount, 2009). The book of Revelation in the Christian Bible even alludes to these tales. Needless to say, Nero did not come back, either alive or resurrected.

Freemasons (1425–)

Long associated with secrecy, little is known about the Freemason's origins, activities, or members. A likely explanation is that they started as a craft guild of master masons (stone workers) who were well-educated professional for their time (Cryer, 2006) Regardless, formal Masonic lodges were noted in England during the 1700s (Knoop & Jones, 1947). A number of famous people have been assumed to be Freemasons, including about one-third of American presidents (masonicfind.com). Perhaps the fact that the Freemasons, their membership, and their rituals are shrouded in secrecy makes them susceptible to many conspiracy theories.

One of the more interesting conspiracy theories surrounding the Freemasons is that many United States presidents and many of the symbols of the United States reflect Masonic symbols. Both Ben Franklin and George Washington were Freemasons (Hodapp & Von Kannon, 2008), and they are considered two of the founders of the United States. A visit to http://cuttingedge.org/n1040.html discusses the prevalence of Masonic imagery (and its purported connections to Lucifer) in some detail. Apparently, the architect responsible for the layout of Washington, DC, one Pierre Charles L'Enfante, hid occult symbols throughout the District including:

- Dupont, Logan, and Scott Circles form the top points of the Devil's Pentagram.

- Not only do these circles form the Devil's Pentagram, they form the number 666 (also associated with the Devil).
- The Washington Monument is an obelisk inside a circle, which represents the Egyptian sun god Ra, and supposedly the Bible specifically states that the sun god is Satan.

We can scoff over some of these connections and the idea that the Freemasons deliberately set up the United States (and Washington, DC), but this conspiracy theory has made its way into our popular culture, as evidenced by such movies as *National Treasure*.

Conspiracy theories allege that the Freemasons have been up to more nefarious doings then simply messing with Washington, DC's traffic. Some say that Freemasons work with the Illuminati to try to establish the New World Order (Berlet & Lyons, 2000). The militant Palestinian organization called Hamas believes that the Freemasons are a secret society of Jews seeking world domination. Alternatively, the Freemasons are purported to be originators or at least supporters of communism (Makow, 2022). During New Hampshire tax protests in the early 2000s, Edward Lewis Brown and Elaine Alice Brown claimed that federal income tax was a Freemason, Illuminati, and Zionist plot to gain control of America, and ultimately the world (Senz, 2007).

Conspiracy theorists would also argue that the Freemasons are behind a variety of other events. For example, supposedly they faked the moon landing, a belief that is supported by some Masonic symbols used by NASA, with the additional belief that NASA is hiding the "fact" that the earth is not a sphere but flat (Dubay, 2014). Other extreme beliefs are that a race of humanoid reptiles is responsible for both the Freemasons and the Illuminati, that Jack the Ripper was a Freemason (theconspiracyblog.com.), and that President Kennedy was killed by the Freemasons (Hodapp & Von Kannon, 2008).

The Illuminati (1700s–)

The Illuminati show up in many conspiracy theories, believed to be a secret society that works toward world domination. They figure prominently in New World Order conspiracy theories for nearly three centuries. The Illuminati began around 1776 as a Bavarian secret society, working toward the separation of church and state, eradication of superstition, and limiting state abuses of power (van Dülmen, 1992). They were outlawed in the late 1700s along with the Freemasons and other secret societies, and later blamed for the French Revolution (le Forestier, 1914). While the actual Illuminati secret society did not last into the 1800s, popular culture and myth has suggested their involvement in many historical events (Barkun, 2003; Sykes, 2009).

For example, conservative pundit Rush Limbaugh claimed that President Barack Obama is a member of the Illuminati ("The Barack Obama Illuminati Connection," 2009). However, *Playboy* magazine published the suggestion that the Illuminati conspiracy was really based on a 1960s practical joke by a group called the Discordians (Galer, 2020).

MODERN-AGE CONSPIRACY THEORIES

John F. Kennedy (1963)

Cloward (2013) suggests that the modern age of the conspiracy theory began the day that the thirty-fifth president, John F. Kennedy, was assassinated on November 22, 1963, in Dallas, Texas. His presidency, while characterized by hope, was also a tense time for the United States with an escalating cold war with the Soviet Union, the failed Bay of Pigs invasion, and the Cuban missile crisis occurring in the months prior to his assassination. Very shortly after his death, conspiracy theories about it began to swirl ("Findings: Report of the Select Committee on Assassinations," 2016), even while the Warren Commission was assigned the task of investigating the assassination. While the Warren Commission concluded that Lee Harvey Oswald was a lone assassin (Hunter, 1978), conspiracy theorists still place the blame for Kennedy's death on various groups and agencies.

For some conspiracy theorists, operatives with ties to New Orleans were responsible for the assassination (Malouse, 2013), as covered in hearings after the assassination held by the Warren Commission and a House Select Committee. One idea was that it was an assassination at the behest of Mob boss Carlos Marcello to prevent his deportation to Guatemala (Lewis, 2016). Another idea proposed in the Warren Commission hearings about the assassination was that it had something to do with Lee Harvey Oswald's activism on behalf of the pro-Cuba organization called Fair Play for Cuba, of which he was the only New Orleans branch member. Alternatively, it may have been arranged by the anti-Castro group called the Cuban Revolutionary Council, which was also housed in New Orleans. Finally, conspiracy theorists have proposed that while Oswald was living in New Orleans, he was involved with the Central Intelligence Agency (CIA) in a plot to develop chemical weapons to assassinate Fidel Castro (Baker, 2010).

While ultimately the Warren Commission determined that the CIA was not involved in Kennedy's assassination, John Newman, a former military intelligence officer and National Security Agency operative, claimed that both the CIA and the FBI not only tampered with evidence, but that CIA agent James Angleton was responsible for the assassination, with or without CIA director,

Allen Dulles. The CIA was also believed to be working with both the Mafia and anti-Castro Cubans in the United States, and all three of these groups were unhappy with Kennedy's view that the best way to get along with the Soviet Union, and with Castro's Cuba, was to engage in a strategy of appeasement (Ventura, 2013).

Conspiracy theorists also proposed that other government-linked agents were behind Kennedy's assassination. For example, James W. Douglass argued that Kennedy was killed because he was de-escalating tensions with the Soviet Union, which was not good for interests of the military or businesses that supplied the military (Anderson, 2008). The Secret Service was also said to be complicit in the assassination in that they failed to provide adequate protection (Palamara, 1997), or that they deliberately destroyed records of Kennedy's trips in the months prior to the assassination (Assassination Records Review Board, 1995).

A final conspiracy of note involves Kennedy's successor, Lyndon Baines Johnson. Supposedly, Johnson did not like the Kennedys and believed Kennedy would remove him from the vice president slot on the 1964 election ticket (Kroth, 2013). This theory was first floated less than three years after Kennedy's assassination (Holland, 2004) in a letter written by Lee Harvey Oswald's killer, Jack Ruby. Joachim Joesten, a German journalist and the author of *The Dark Side of Lyndon Baines Johnson*, was credited as being the first conspiracy theorist to tie Johnson to the assassination. Joesten (2013) linked Johnson to other players in the various conspiracy theories associated with Kennedy's assassination, including the CIA, FBI, the Secret Service, and the Dallas oligarchy.

New World Order (1970s–1990s)

The term "New World Order" has legitimate origins—early in the twentieth century, major political figures used the term to describe shifting geopolitical boundaries and balance of power following World War I and World War II (Knock, 2019). In the early 1970s, however, the term took on more sinister meaning. Conservative Gary Allen published several books purporting a global conspiracy, including the "None Dare Call It Conspiracy" that claimed that international banking groups controlled US domestic political and economic activities. Then President George H. W. Bush even used the term in a speech to Congress, titled "Toward a New World Order" (Zanella, 2018), ironically delivered on September 11, 1990, eleven years before the September 11, 2001, bombing of the Twin Towers, an event that itself is the subject of multiple conspiracy theories.

Apparently, Bush's use of the term riled up the Christian Right, and the 1990s saw many conspiracy theories spring up in response to Bush's inadvertent use of a term, that was probably *not* meant to imply some sort of global takeover. Leading the charge was Pat Robertson (1991), an American televangelist and author, who proposed in his book *The New World Order* that Wall Street and foreign agents were secretly encouraging a global government to further the interests of the Antichrist (Barkun, 2003). Fear of the New World Order is believed to have given impetus to the right-wing militia and anti-government movements of the 1990s (Pitcavage, 2001). The Denver airport, built in 1995, was believed to be the headquarters for the New World Order, with conspiracy theorists pointing to its size and artwork as proof that it is more than just an airport (Marrs, 2013).

Moon Landing (1976–)

The first manned moon landing occurred with Apollo 11 on July 20, 1960. Despite considerable evidence that the moon landing really did occur (Than, 2009), conspiracy theories began circulating not long after the event. One of the first proponents of a moon landing conspiracy theory was Bill Kaysing (2002), a former Navy officer. In his 1976 book *We Never Went to the Moon: America's Thirty Billion Dollar Swindle*, he claimed that the chance of the first mission being successful was well below .002 percent, arguing that it would have been much easier to fake it (the moon landing) than make it. Walt Disney was supposed to be behind the fake, hiring famed director Stanley Kubrick to direct the event (Schadewald, 1980)

Why would the United States fake the moon landings? Some conspiracy theorists claim that space race competition with the Soviet Union was so fierce that the United States felt compelled to win, so the moon landings were faked to prove the United States had a more advanced space program than the Soviet Union (Plait, 2002). Others claimed that the moon landing was faked by NASA because they were spending billions of dollars on a space/moon landing program and needed something to show for it to keep the money flowing (Kaysing, 2002). Some even argued that a faked moon landing provided a convenient distraction from the disaster of the Vietnam War, claiming that it was no coincidence that NASA spent less money on moon landings as the war wound down ("Was the Apollo Moon Landing Fake?," 2009).

Regardless of their reasoning, from 6–20 percent of Americans, about 25 percent of Britons, and almost 50 percent of Russians believe the first moon landing was fake (Osborne, 2020). Some celebrities have publicly supported these conspiracies, including actress Marion Cotillard, comedian Richard Belzer, and actress Whoopi Goldberg (Hanson, 2019).

The Majestic 12 (1980s)

One of the more popular conspiracy theories concerning unidentified flying objects (UFOs) or extraterrestrial visitations to Earth involves the "Majestic 12," a secret group supposedly formed in 1947 under executive order by then President Harry Truman (Donovan, 2011). However, it did not become part of the UFO conspiracy lexicon until the 1980s, when Timothy Good claimed that he had gained possession of documents from the Truman administration that described the crash of a spaceship in Roswell, New Mexico (Knight, 2003). Supposedly these documents included evidence of the existence of a small, gray humanoid alien, as well as a video interview with the "visitor" (Goldberg, 2008).

Who were the members of this secret society, the Majestic 12, supposedly brought together to keep the secret of extraterrestrial visitors from the public? The group included scientists (Lloyd Berkner, Detlev Bronk, Vannevar Bush, and Donald Howard Menzel) and high-ranking military officers (James Forrestal, Gordon Gray, Roscoe Hillenkoetter, Jerome Hunsaker, Robert Montague, Sidney Souers, Nathan Twining, and Hoyt Vandenberg), many of whom had ties to the Air Force, CIA, and other government agencies (Frazier, 2010). Interestingly, the Majestic 12 has been proposed to be a misinformation campaign (a sort of strategic conspiracy theory) propagated by the US government to deflect public attention away from other secret projects of the Air Force (Frazier, 2010).

FEMA Camps (1982)

The Federal Emergency Management Agency (FEMA) is a government agency developed to assist in disasters (Graff, 2017). While conspiracy theories about FEMA concentration camps are still active today, they got their start in the early 1980s, when the far-right anti-government militia group, Posse Comitatus, warned its supporters that FEMA was creating concentration camps supposedly to detain so-called hardcore patriots (Keller, 2010).

Unlike many of the conspiracy theories discussed in this book that are more likely to have proponents with more right-wing, conservative political affiliation, individuals from both the right and left may believe that, in the event of a disaster, FEMA will be mobilized and incarcerate US citizens in concentration camps to control their actions (Keller, 2010). For example, one of the most extreme examples from the left comes from an animal liberation website, Negotiation Is Over, that claims the US military was working with FEMA to round up dissenters and put them into camps (Nelson, 2011).

However, the majority of believers in FEMA concentration camps are from the far-right, anti-government, doomsday "prepper" community. For example, the Militia of Montana claimed that FEMA was building concentration camps in the Northern Cascade mountains (Neiwert, 2009). Also, a military training operation called "Jade Helm 15" was believed to be preparation for an internment camp in Texas (Smith, 2015). Additionally, and as testimony to the dangerous nature of conspiracy theories, the Las Vegas shooter who killed over fifty concertgoers in 2017, believed in a number of anti-government conspiracy theories including the FEMA concentration camp idea (Wilson, 2018).

Chemtrails (1999)

Conspiracy theories about chemicals sprayed from the air arose following a 1996 report by the US States Air Force concerning weather modification, and it morphed into the idea that the Air Force was spraying its citizens with mysterious chemicals, "chemtrails," to control them (Smith, 2013). Some conspiracists claim that the chemtrails are part of a global conspiracy rather than just a conspiracy by the US Air Force. One idea is that the Illuminati or some other group sprayed people to test bioweapons, for population control, or to increase drug company profits by making people sick (Fraser, 2009). Others argue that the chemtrails are part of an elaborate electromagnetic weapons program (Poladian, 2013).

While it may be easy to dismiss those who believe frozen condensation trails are actually toxic chemicals or other agents of malfeasance, the US Congress considered action called "The Space Preservation Act of 2001" to prohibit space weapons, and they included chemtrails in their list of weapons that would be banned. Conspiracy theorists from other countries jumped on the bandwagon, and these include Canada, where citizens circulated a signed petition against air-born sprayings that could affect the health of Canadian citizens ("37th Parliament, 2nd Sessions Edited Hansard: Number 100," 2003). Additionally, a United Kingdom Minister of State was asked to address what his department was doing to mediate the effects of aircraft chemtrails (Simons, 2013).

CONCLUSION

Clearly, conspiracy theories are not a new phenomenon. They have been around throughout recorded human history. The present chapter reviewed early conspiracy beliefs, many of which are within the living memory of US citizens (such as those about the JFK assassination, the moon landing, chemtrails), as well as those that seem to live on in popular culture (such as those about the Freemasons and the Illuminati). However, one characteristic that distinguishes these early conspiracy theories from the more bizarre theories of the twenty-first century reviewed in the next chapter, is that they often appear more understandable or reasonable. As an example, for people who lived during a time when Queen Victoria's grandchildren ruled virtually every European country, it may have seemed reasonable to believe that a secret group of the rich and powerful controlled the world. Also, for US citizens who were alive before the time of automobiles or airplanes, surely it would boggle the mind to imagine humans going from riding horses to flying to the moon. Additionally, given the sheer number of Secret Service and police on duty in Dallas on that November day in 1963, it may have seemed impossible that one person could fire one bullet that killed the president. Finally, when the first commercial jet planes flew across America, who could blame people for wondering just what exactly were those trails left in the sky?

Another characteristic that distinguishes these early conspiracies from those prominent after the twenty-first century is that they tended to spread slowly due to the limited telecommunication technology of their day. However, the rise of the internet and social media (especially Facebook) has so exploded the proliferation of more contemporary conspiracy beliefs, that one would be hard pressed to find anyone who has not heard about, believed in, or disseminated some conspiracy theories at some point.

Chapter 4

Contemporary
Conspiracy Theories

We have chosen to identify contemporary conspiracy theories as those circulating after the September 11, 2001, terrorist attacks in New York, at the Pentagon, and in Pennsylvania. Our reasons for marking this period as the cut-off point were that we began a new millennium, social media and the internet became prominent, and an extremely high-impact event occurred at the beginning of this new millennium—the 9/11 attacks on the US World Trade Centers. We present our review of contemporary conspiracy theories in roughly chronological order, beginning with beliefs about the 9/11 attacks, then covering other beliefs (2000–2022), then ending with beliefs about two of the most recent and high-impact events—the COVID-19 pandemic and the 2020 US presidential election. Most conspiracy beliefs we cover in this chapter are primarily relevant to the United States, but some have more international relevance, and still others focus on specific public figures.

However, even for conspiracy beliefs that originated from specific locations, the speed and wide reach of the internet has often allowed them to have global impact. For example, while the attacks of 9/11 were limited to US soil, the increasing fear and attendant security spread internationally. Also, concerns about climate-related disasters, oil spills, and airplane crashes often prompt widespread speculation as to their causes and meaning. Additionally, conspiracy theories about specific celebrities may come to have a wider purpose, such as when the deaths of musicians and actors are linked to supposed child-trafficking schemes by liberals, or when public figures are discredited as being fraudulent or even doppelgangers (Bartleet, 2017). In any case, the wide range of conspiracy theories we review in this chapter seem to have exploded into the new millennium, as a testament to the power of the internet and social media.

CONSPIRACY BELIEFS CONCERNING
THE 9/11 ATTACKS

For many of us, images of the suicide bombings that took place on the morning of September 11, 2001, are still fresh in our minds. However, it has been over twenty years, and many young adults today have no first-person memories of what happened. During the event, four well-coordinated terrorist attacks struck the northeastern United States around 9 a.m., with hijacked planes crashing into both the north and south towers of the World Trade Center in Manhattan, with another plane crashing into the Pentagon building in Virginia, and with a fourth plane crashing in rural eastern Pennsylvania, apparently diverted from its intended target in Washington, DC, by a passenger revolt (Janos, 2020). The Islamic group al-Qaeda claimed responsibility (Moghadam, 2008), and the event led to the War on Terror and a US invasion of Afghanistan, which did not end until 2021 with the Doha Agreement in which the United States withdrew its forces (Putz, 2021).

The initial 9/11 conspiracy theories first appeared in Europe, exemplified by the French journalist, Thierry Meyssan in a book, *L'Effroyable Imposture or 9/11: The Big Lie in English Speaking Countries* (Rosenthal, 2010). Other national news outlets, including *Le Monde* and *Die Tageszeitung* published various conspiracy theories (Knight, 2008), but these were mostly ignored in the United States. Some celebrities have expressed skepticism about either the attacks or the official US government version of the attacks, and Collins (2021) has identified nine entertainment giants who have been, in his words, "9/11 Conspiracy Truthers." These include Woody Harrelson and Marion Cotillard, who have claimed that the government's investigation was flawed and that it has offered misleading information. Charlie Sheen and Matthew Bellamy have blamed Washington, DC, itself for the attacks, and Mark Ruffalo, Rosie O'Donnell, and Martin Sheen have expressed doubts about the mechanics of the plane attacks during 9/11.

However, conspiracy theories about 9/11 actually gained steam a few years after the attacks, perhaps because of disillusionment with President George W. Bush and/or his war in Afghanistan (Knight, 2008). Broadly speaking, these theories follow various narratives:

(1) The US government knew the attacks were coming but let them happen anyway.
(2) Persons within the US government were responsible for planning the attacks.
(3) Official accounts of the attacks by the US government are inaccurate.

One of the most common 9/11 conspiracy theories is that, at least to some degree, the United States knew that the attacks were going to happen but did nothing to stop them. A member of the UK Prime Minister Tony Blair's government (Michael Meacher) even publicly stated that the United States had failed to prevent the attacks, even though they knew there were going to happen (MacAskill, 2003). As evidence for this advance knowledge, some conspiracists note that money was being made by insider trading of stocks for both United Airlines and American Airlines in the days leading up to the attacks (Poteshman, 2006). Other companies, including insurance giant Travelers and the investment firms of Morgan Stanley, Fidelity Investments, and TD Waterhouse also saw unusually high levels of trading in the days just before the attacks ("Profiting from Disaster?," 2001). Still other conspiracies propose that the US Air Force was ordered to stand down on September 11, 2001 (Aaronovitch, 2009), that Israel knew beforehand that the attack was going to happen ("Were Israelis Detained on Sept. 11 Spies?," 2002).

The second cluster of 9/11 conspiracies suggest that the United States itself was behind the attacks rather than al-Qaeda, or perhaps that it was not an attack at all, but a controlled demolition. For example, a physicist from Brigham Young University was among the group "Architects and Engineers for 9/11 Truth" (AE911Truth), which claims that the aircraft alone were insufficient to bring down the towers (Blatchford, 2010). Academics from the University of Copenhagen and Brigham Young University stated that thermite (used in explosives, but not jet fuel) was found at the site of the Twin Towers (Dean, 2006). Others point to missiles launched by the United States itself, attacking its own people, such as Meyssan (2002), who claims that it was not an airplane that struck the Pentagon, but rather a missile, because the hole in the Pentagon was too small to have been caused by a Boeing 757. One of President George W. Bush's own economists suggested that there were no planes involved, claiming that they were actually missiles disguised by holograms or other computer-generated imaging (CGI) technology to look like airplanes (Henley, 2002).

The third cluster of 9/11 conspiracy theories acknowledge that the attacks were the work of hostile foreign agents, but they claim that the United States either bungled or deliberately misconstrued the course of events. According to the "9/11 Commission" report, the black boxes from flights 77 and 93 were recovered, but one of them was too badly damaged to yield anything ("United 93: Full Transcript," 2006). Also, two men who helped federal agents retrieve the black boxes claimed that one of the boxes found later "went missing" (Swanson, 2003). A German professor proposed that the American translators who transcribed the Bin Laden video tapes (in which he allegedly claims to have known the facts of the attacks ahead of time) translated them inaccurately (Morris, 2001). Others claim that the person in the video is not Bin

Laden at all, based on differences in his appearance from other photos, and from his wearing of jewelry, which is forbidden by Muslim law ("Osama Tape Appears Fake, Experts Conclude," 2006). Lastly, and perhaps most frightening, is the conspiracy theory that the CIA and its then director George Tenet actively recruited two of the hijackers, then conducted a coverup to keep the US government in the dark about their relationship to the two men (Shenon, 2011).

OTHER CONTEMPORARY CONSPIRACY THEORIES (2000–2022)

Global Warming (2002)

Despite statements by worldwide scientists (Biello, 2010) that human-caused changes to the earth's climate contribute to recent decreases in snow and ice, rising sea levels, extreme fluctuations in temperature, and other natural disasters, conspiracy theories about climate change continue to thrive. These conspiracy theories have taken aim at both scientists and politicians. For example, one idea proposed is that the scientists are using flawed data (Simons, 2013). Even worse, the Lavoisier Group (an Australian organization mostly comprising engineers and businesspeople) and later the Cooler Heads Coalition (based in the United States and operated by the Competitive Enterprise Institute) have claimed that researchers "tweaked" their data because no one would be interested in results that were not alarming (Gross, 2007), or that such nonalarming results would jeopardize the researchers ongoing research funding (McKie, 2019). Finally, Uscinsky, Douglas, and Lewandowsky (2017) note that some conspiracists believe the peer-review process to be corrupt, focusing less on the goal of valid scientific findings and more on the goal of stifling dissent.

Other conspiracy theorists propose that climate change is not the invention of self-serving scientists, but rather a form of political manipulation. For example, Douglas and Sutton (2015) describe how a professor of atmospheric science suggested that global warming served the political purpose of giving the United States an enemy, since it lacked one after the Cold War with the Soviet Union (ignoring, presumably, al-Qaeda). Other conspiracists believed that supporters of the Kyoto Protocol (the 1992 international treaty to reduce greenhouse gasses) were hell-bent on establishing a global governance (see the US Senate Committee on Environment and Public Works at http://epw .senate.gov/speechitem.cfm?party=rep&id=263759). Still others claimed that the idea of global warming was a leftist hoax to promote the need for a socialist ideology (Uscinski, Douglas, & Lewandowsky, 2017), or that it was a scam by renewable-energy companies (Douglas & Sutton, 2015), or that it is being used to promote nuclear power (Douglas & Sutton, 2015). Former president Donald Trump began claiming in 2012 that China was behind the global warming idea to undermine US manufacturing success (Wong, 2016).

Avril Lavigne (2011)

Canadian pop-punk artist, Avril Lavigne, was the subject of a Brazilian replacement conspiracy theory, circulated via a blog in 2011. The blog, titled "Avril Esta Morta," claimed that she committed suicide in 2003 (or that her supposed death was due to a snowboarding accident), but that because her record company was desperate to continue to benefit from her popularity, they hired a doppelganger named Melissa Vandella to impersonate her (Estatie, 2017). Supporters of this conspiracy claim that her handwriting, physical appearance, and personal style changed, and that in one photo she has a tattoo with the name Melissa written on her hand. However, according to Evon (2015), the rumor of Avril's death and doppelganger was actually a joke on a Brazilian website, designed specifically to illustrate the rapid spread of misinformation on the internet, and how easily conspiracy theories become viral.

Armenian Genocide Denial (Early 2000s)

In the early days of World War I, the Ottoman Empire encroached upon Russian and Persian (Iranian) territory, with Armenians and non-Muslims then marginalized and faced with either forced conversion to Islam or deportation (Maksudyan, 2019). Paramilitary groups also massacred Armenians, ultimately leaving only 200,000 (out of nearly two million) Armenians alive by the end of World War I (Morris & Ze'evi, 2019).While Turkey has long denied the existence of this Armenian Genocide, a "denialism conspiracy belief" gained traction in academia during the early years of the twenty-first century, with claims that the killings never occurred, or that they were a rational response to wartime unrest (Suny, 2015). Some have proposed that these academic writers were fearful of reprisals if they described the extent of the massacre, but denial of the event continues in some recent university publications (Hovannisian, 2015; Suny, 2015).

Weather and Earthquake Control (2005)

The "High-frequency Active Auroral Research Program" (HAARP) is a US project that has been accused of causing a number of weather and natural disasters. HAARP has been around since the 1990s to advance knowledge of the earth's ionosphere, including the role of solar interaction and its effects on radio signals. Even though the Air Force shut down HAARP's official operation in 2014, it is still available for hire to researchers (McCoy, 2015).

Since its inception, HAARP has been the subject of a number of conspiracy theories. For example, a Russian military journal claimed it could flip Earth's magnetic poles (Shachtman, 2009). Former governor of Minnesota and professional wrestler Jesse Ventura speculated that it was being used to control people with radio waves (Baenen, 2013). These theories gained so much traction that two men were arrested late in 2016 for planning to destroy the facility because they believed it could trap people's souls (Zak, 2016).

Barack Obama (2008)

Barack Hussein Obama was the forty-fourth president of the United States, and the first president of color. An article in *Mother Jones* in 2012 charts the many conspiracy theories linked to President Obama, and then debunks them. The article groups these conspiracy beliefs into five categories: (1) that he is a Muslim and/or a terrorist, (2) that he is not a US citizen, (3) that he is a radical leftist, (4) that he is a weirdo at best and pervert at worst, and (5) that he is a power-mad dictator. As a sample, we will describe the first two of these conspiracy clusters.

Rumors that Obama is a secret Muslim/Muslim sympathizer began years before his run for the presidency, back in 2004 when he was running for the US Senate. Perry Bacon, Jr. (2007) notes that rumors, such as Obama being Senator John McCain's illegitimate son, began circulating on conservative news outlets at this time. The government of Iraq got on board the conspiracy train, with one member of parliament claiming that Obama's father was a Shite Muslim (Taylor, 2015). After Obama's swearing in ceremony as president, a chain email claimed that Obama was sworn in using the Qur'an, when it was actually his personal Christian Bible (Holan, 2007). Of course, this was not the only religion-based conspiracy theory surrounding him. For example, *Politifact* noted that one conspiracy theory making the rounds claimed that Obama was the Anti-Christ (Hollyfield, 2008). These conspiracy theories may have been able to gain traction because of xenophobia on the part of many Americans, which particularly targeted Muslims after the 9/11 attack on the Twin Towers in New York and the subsequent military action in Middle Eastern Muslim countries.

Whether propagated by racists or political conservatives, Obama was plagued by "birther" conspiracists beginning in 2008 at the time of his presidential campaign (Jardina & Traugott, 2019; Pasek, Stark, Krosnick, & Tompson, 2015). Birther conspiracies ran the gamut from claiming that his birth certificate was a forgery, that he became an Indonesian citizen as a child, that he was a dual citizen of Kenya and the United States, or that he was actually born in Kenya (his father's birthplace) rather than Hawaii (Tomasky, 2011). Some birther rumors made it to mainstream and quasi-mainstream news outlets, both conservative and liberal. For example, *The Telegraph* (Swaine, 2011) reported that, while the conservatives were spreading the rumor, it originated among Hillary Clinton supporters. A Pennsylvania democrat tried, unsuccessfully, to have Obama removed from the presidential ballot with the claim that he was born in Kenya (Hinkelman 2008), and NPR referred to him as Kenyan-born ("Trial and Triumph: Stories out of Africa," 2008). Even after Obama produced his birth certificate, which clearly showed his birthplace as Oahu, Hawaii, the birther theories continued (Mikkelson, 2011).

Many other more fringe conspiracy theories exist concerning past president Obama. For example, one claim is that when he was a teen, he was a time-traveling tourist on Mars. Another claim is that he won the election through hypnosis. Still another claim is that he removed the US flag from Air Force One and replaced it with his own campaign log.

Deepwater Horizon (2010)

Deepwater Horizon was an oil drilling rig that was run by British Petroleum, owned by Transocean, and built in South Korea. While operating in the Gulf of Mexico, an onboard fire started the night of April 20, 2010, ultimately sinking the rig on the morning of April 22. Nearly a dozen workers were killed (Welch & Joyner, 2010) and the environmental damage was substantial, described by some as the worst environmental disaster in US history ("Gulf of Mexico Oil Leak Worst U.S. Environmental Disaster," 2010).

CBS News reported a number of conspiracy theories that had sprung up in the wake of the Deepwater Horizon disaster (Phillips, 2010). They are truly "equal opportunity" conspiracy theories, with both liberals and conservatives blaming the other for destruction of the rig, and for various nefarious reasons. Some conservative pundits and bloggers, including Rush Limbaugh, claimed that the Obama administration blew up the rig to put a halt to oil Deepwater Horizon's drilling, or to revive the Kerry–Lieberman "Cap and Trade" that regulated industrial carbon dioxide emissions. In his broadcast, Phillips also noted that the liberal left placed the blame for the Deepwater Horizon disaster squarely in the hands of former vice president Dick Cheney, claiming that Cheney's former employer Halliburton used below-standard concrete in the rig, intending to boost oil prices with the shortages that resulted after Deepwater Horizon's demise.

Foreign governments and agents were not immune from accusation. For example, one claim was that North Korea sent a mini submarine to attack the rig (Phillips, 2010). Why? That question has yet to be answered. Even the Judeo-Christian God was not immune from speculation, with a Baptist preacher from Florida proposing that Obama's treatment of Israel led to God punishing him with the disaster of Deepwater Horizon (Phillips, 2010).

Malala Yousafzai (2012)

Malala Yousafzai is a well-known Pakistani activist for women and winner of the Nobel Peace Prize. To most, she is known as the young woman who was shot by the Taliban but recovered to fight its extremism. However, she is also the subject of a conspiracy theory that, as with the Avril Lavigne doppelganger theory, started as a hoax. The satirical paper *Dawn*, with a headline stating that the article was a *piece of satire*, published a report that Malala was not in fact a Pakistani school girl, but a Caucasian from Poland (Paracha, 2013).

Perhaps the most extreme conspiracy theory concerning Malala Yousafzai is that she not only engineered her own shooting, but that she was a CIA plant. According to *The Atlantic*, a member of Pakistan's leading religious political party suggested that she was created by America "to promote their own culture of nudity and to defame Pakistan around the world" (John, 2013). Also, some Pakistanis called her "Malala Dramazai," or a drama queen who staged her own shooting to get a visa out of Pakistan and into a western country.

Crisis Actors (2012)

Outside of conspiracy theories, "crisis actors" are actually trained individuals who may be employed for disaster simulations used in the training of first responders. However, as a conspiracy theory, such "crisis actors" were supposedly plants by the government for the purpose of expanding their political goals (Koebler, 2018). For example, conspiracy theories surrounding the shootings at Sandy Hook and Parkland schools, as well as the Boston Marathon bombing, claim that the US government used actors to portray victims, survivors, bystanders, and emergency response personal to cause panic and fear so that they could legislate the reduction of private gun ownership and the expansion of government surveillance of its citizens (Yglesias ,2018).

Sandy Hook (2012)

In mid-December of 2012, Adam Lanza of Newtown, Connecticut, went on a shooting spree, first killing his mother, then twenty students and six staff at Sandy Hook Elementary School, later committing suicide via self-inflicted gunshot wound. Despite the tragic nature and graphic news footage of the massacre, a number of conspiracy theories arose almost immediately, both within and outside of the United States, the most egregious of which claimed that it never happened. This idea was popularized by Alex Jones in his radio broadcasts, with claims that Sandy Hook was a false flag operation staged by gun control advocates in the Obama-era US government to push through gun control legislation (McCarson, 2012). In 2022, a jury required Alex Jones to pay over 49 million dollars in punitive damages to Sandy Hook parents. The state media outlet of Iran even jumped on this conspiracy theory bandwagon, claiming that Israeli death squads were responsible for the shooting at Sandy Hook (Moynihan, 2012). As an example that conspiracy ideation crosses socioeconomic and educational conditions, a Florida Atlantic University former professor, James Tracy, claimed that for political reasons, a coverup had occurred concerning the details of the Sandy Hook shooting (Tracy, 2012).

Pope Benedict XVI (2013)

Pope Benedict XVI (born Joseph Aloisius Ratzinger) was pope only from 2005 until he resigned in 2013, the first pope to resign in 600 years. The official reason given for his resignation was poor health, but considerable speculation occurred in both ecclesial and lay circles that Benedict did not, in fact, resign voluntarily. If Pope Benedict's resignation was coerced in some way, then his successor (Pope Francis) would not truly be the pope because the only recognized papal resignation is one that is taken without pressure (Chandler, 2015). Why might Benedict have been pressured to resign? According to one theory, it might have been due to conflict over Catholic church reforms such as increased transparency about the sex scandals facing the church, or over management of the Vatican bank (Chandler, 2015). Some of the former Pope Benedict's actions may have added to speculation about his resignation, such as his choice to continue wearing papal white and to have a surrogate defend him with the press.

Paul Walker (2013)

Paul Walker was an American actor most famous for his role in the *Fast and the Furious* franchise, who died in a high-speed car crash in November of 2013. Police noted that Walker (with a passenger) was traveling up to ninety-three miles per hour when he crashed. They saw no signs that Walker had been drag racing, and they determined that the most likely cause of the fatal accident was the speed of travel and the age of his tires (Duke, 2014). When Walker crashed, he was returning from charity foundation event, Reach Out Worldwide, for which he was raising money for victims of Typhoon Haiyan (Duke & Sutton, 2013). According to a Facebook post, Walker's car was tampered with because he was planning to expose the Clinton Foundation as a charitable organization with crimes against children in Haiti (Putterman, 2020).

Malaysia Airlines Flight MH370 (2014)

Malaysia Airlines flight MH370 was operating between Kuala Lumpur and Beijing, when it deviated from its planned course and disappeared over the Indian Ocean (MacLeod, Winter, & Gray, 2014). The aircraft and its passengers, mostly Chinese nationals, have never been found ("MH370 Search: Mozambique Debris Almost Certainly from Missing Plane," 2016). While the cause of the plane's disappearance has not been definitively established, suggestions have included a power interruption in the plane during flight (Sydne, 2014), or an explosion from the 10,000 pounds of lithium-ion batteries the plane had in its cargo hold ("Safety Worries Lead U.S. Airline to Ban Battery Shipments," 2015; "Factual Information, Safety Investigation: Malaysia Airlines MH370Boeing 777-220ER," 2014–; Jansen, 2013; Knowler, 2015), or some other cause of sudden decompression leading to hypoxia for the crew and loss of control of the plane ("MH370—Definition of Underwater Search Areas," 2014). Another speculation was that the plane was the target of terrorists, particularly because two passengers boarded the plane with passports that had been reported stolen (Fuller & Schmitt, 2014). Shortly after the incident, financial records of the crew were also examined as a possible motive (Gardner & Fisher, 2014), with the US Federal Bureau of Investigation (FBI) getting involved to the point of interviewing the captain's wife (Collins, 2014).

More fringe theories involving the disappearance of MH370 also developed. For example, because friends and relatives of the missing passengers could still reach their loved ones' cell phones, and the passengers continued to be logged in to their Chinese social media accounts, some conspiracists speculated that the passengers had been the victims of a mass kidnapping or supernatural event (Frizell, 2014; Wan & Liu, 2014). Bloggers suggested a Bermuda Triangle–like mystery, with aliens abducting a plane and all its contents, and the social media platform Reddit was abuzz with the coincidence of the numbers three and seven—with Flight 370 disappearing on 3/7, traveling 3,700 kilometers, at an altitude of 37,000 feet, with one traveler aged 37, and with Malaysia Airlines typically flying 37,000 passengers every day. It was also the thirty-seventh month since the Japanese nuclear reactor at Fukushima was damaged in a tsunami, with the reactor located at the thirty-seventh parallel, with thirty-seven injuries occurring. Conspiracists concluded that the MH370 tragedy was somehow preordained and meant to be. Another idea proposed on Reddit was that Kim Jong-Un of North Korea was responsible for the plane's loss to replicate a North Korean plane hijacking in 1969. Finally, of course, the Illuminati or extraterrestrials were accused of manipulating the energy grid and bringing down MH370 (Frizell, 2014).

Malaysia Airlines Flight MH17 (2014)

Another plane operated by Malaysia Airlines, MH17, went down in Ukraine only four months after MH370 disappeared. Nearly 300 passengers and crew died in this crash, which originated in Amsterdam and was going to Kuala Lumpur (Mullen, 2014). The Dutch Safety Board had responsibility for investigation of the crash, concluding that the plane had been shot down by a surface to air missile launched from a section of the Ukraine that was controlled by Russian separatists (Smith-Spark & Masters, 2018). While the Russian government denied any involvement (Sipalan 2019), the governments of two countries whose citizens were among the bulk of the victims (Holland, Australia) placed culpability firmly upon the Russian government ("MH17: The Netherlands and Australia Hold Russia Responsible," 2018).

As with MH370, conspiracy theories quickly began to swirl around the event, focusing not on *whether* the plane was shot down, but *by whom*. Reidy (2014) has described five main speculations for the responsible group. As with the loss of MH370, the Illuminati were accused of shooting down the plane because they supposedly have an affinity for the number seven and for multiples of seven—so they shot down flight MH17, which was a Boeing 777, in the seventh month of 2014, which includes a multiple of seven. Another conspiracy theory concerning the Illuminati (or the "Global Elite") suggested that the many AIDS/HIV researchers on the flight were the target by governments because their pharmaceutical industries did not want a cure for AIDS/HIV to be discovered (Haven, 2014), and because the Global Elite was to keep AIDS around to depopulate the earth (Reidy, 2014).

Another conspiracy theory about the crash of MH17 was linked with Russia's long- standing (and rapidly intensifying at the time of this writing) feud with Ukraine. One speculation is that the Ukrainian Army actually shot down the plane, rather than the Russian separatists in Ukraine (Reidy, 2014), although these conspiracists have yet to offer a reason why the Ukrainian Army would benefit from shooting down a foreign aircraft. In another version of the theory that Ukraine was to blame for the loss of MH17, Interfax news (a Russian independent news agency) reported that Russian president Vladimir Putin's plane was carrying him from Rio de Janeiro back to Moscow, with very similar coordinates, and only thirty minutes after the MH17 plane's flight ("Reports That Putin Flew Similar Route as MH17, Presidential Airport Says Hasn't Overflown Ukraine for Long Time," 2014). This conspiracy theory again blames Ukraine for shooting down MH17, but this time with a motive—killing Vladimir Putin (Reidy, 2014). However, Ukraine was not the only country targeted with conspiracy theories about it and the loss of MH17. For example, Iran's *Press TV* claimed that Israel was responsible for the fate of MH17, airing an interview with the University of Minnesota professor and Holocaust denier, James Henry Fetzer, in which he claims that Israel's Benhamin Netanyahu was responsible for both MH17 and MH370, hiding the MH370 plane on a British island in the Indian Ocean (Kamm, 2014).

Turkish Conspiracy Theories

Turkey has been identified as a country often plagued by "fake news" stories (Akyol, 2016), and particularly since the rise of President Erdogan's "Justice and Development Party," conspiracy theories have thrived in Turkish politics (Akyol, 2016). For example, the International Mass Media Agency ("Mayor of Ankara has linked the earthquake with conspiracy against Turkey," 2017) reports that the mayor of Ankara attributed an earthquake in 2017 as being generated by hostile governments, and the United States was blamed for other earthquakes ("ABD nin Deprem Silahi HAARP 17," 2017). Other conspiracy theories have been circulated in Turkey that involve foreign powers attempting to disrupt the Turkish government, economy, and society (Danforth, 2014; O'Brien, 2018). One example was when a Turkish anti-terrorism unit found a dead bird in Gazlantep that was believed to have been fitted with a microchip by Israel to spy on Turkey ("Renegade Bird Accused of Being an Israeli Spy Cleared After Careful Examination in Turkey," 2013), although the bird was later alive, given medical treatment, and released. Also, the Turkish prime minister claimed that Israel's 2018 win of the Eurovision song contest was a plot by Jerusalem to stoke interreligious conflict. Finally, one of the more interesting conspiracy theories circulated in Turkey was that ripped jeans were not actually a fashion statement, but a means of communication used between enemy states and their sympathizers within Turkey ("Geheimbotschaften in der Jeanshose," 2017).

Thuli Madonsela (2014)

Thuli Madonsela was a professor of law in South Africa who helped draft South Africa's constitution (Resume of Thuli Madonsela, n.d.), and who was appointed by then President Zuma to serve as the Public Protector of South African democracy (Bathembu, 2009). During her seven-year tenure, she investigated a number of cases involving malfeasance by South African politicians, including the excess spending on President Zuma's lavish private home (Marrian, 2014). Needless to say, President Zuma and the ruling party of South Africa did not take kindly to her report (de Vos, 2014), which was titled "Secure in Comfort." The ruling African National Congress concluded that Madonsela, their appointed Public Protector, was involved in a plot with the Economic Freedom Fighters of South Africa, or the CIA of the United States, with the goal of destabilizing the South African government (Evans, 2021; Rabkin, 2015).

George Soros (2016)

For years, far right groups in the United States have targeted George Soros, the Hungarian American billionaire and philanthropist, claiming that he manipulates world governments and economies. For example, he has been accused of being responsible for the Central American immigrant caravans; the activism of the victims of the school shooting in Parkland, Florida; the "Pussy Hat" marches in cities across the United States against sexual harassment; efforts to discredit Brett Kavanaugh's nomination to the Supreme Court; and establishment of the fact-finding website Snopes (Rizzo, 2018; Shane, Vogel, & Kingsley, 2018).

Some heads of state have joined the legions of Soros detractors. For example, then President Donald Trump tweeted that Soros was behind the protests against Kavanaugh and the immigrant caravans (Jamieson, 2018; Levin, 2018). Icelandic Progressive Prime Minister Gunnlaugsson claimed that Soros was behind a conspiracy to get him removed from power ("Segir Panama-skjölin runnin undan rifjum Soros," 2016). Even Turkey's President Erdogan claimed Soros masterminded the Gezi incidents of civil unrest in Turkey in 2013 as part of his supposed plan to divide and shatter nations (Kucukgocmen & Solaker, 2018).

Seth Rich (2016)

Seth Rich was an employee of the Democratic National Committee, working on developing an App to help voters locate polling places (Morton, 2016). In July of 2016 he was shot to death near his home in Washington, DC (Stein, 2016). Police reported that he may have been killed in a robbery, and many neighbors stated that there had been recent robberies in the neighborhood (Stein, 2016). However, Rich's mother told the media that there appeared to have been a struggle, and that he had not been robbed, but only killed (Collins & Swalec, 2016).

As so often happens, conspiracy theories surrounding the event got their start on social media, with claims that Rich's killing was linked to leaked DNC emails to Wikileaks, or to the FBI investigation into the Clinton Foundation (Whitehouse, 2017). Right-wing conspiracy enthusiasts linked his murder to the so-called Clinton body count of suspicious deaths of individuals close to

President Bill Clinton and Hillary Clinton. These theories really gained steam when mainstream conservative media outlets started repeating them, such as by Fox News pundit Sean Hannity (Collins & Alba, 2019). Ultimately, fact-checking websites determined that no evidence existed to support Rich as the person leaking emails to Wikileaks, or to his death being part of a greater conspiracy (Carroll, 2017; Kiely, 2017; Palma, 2017).

Sutherland Springs Church Shooting (2017)

One Sunday in early November of 2017, Devin Kelly, a former member of the US Air Force, opened fire on the congregation of the First Baptist Church in Sutherland Springs, Texas (Andone, Hartung, & Simon, 2017; Barnitz, 2017). Yelling "Everybody dies, motherfuckers!" he emptied about 700 rounds of ammunition in about eleven minutes, killing twenty-six persons including eight members of one family, and injuring twenty-two ("Texas Shooting Death Toll Includes Unborn Child," 2017; Medina & Spriester, 2018). Investigators initially attributed Kelly's motive to a family dispute ("Texas Officials: Mass Shooting Not Motivated by Religion or Race," 2017), although he had apparently expressed strong anti-religious views on social media platforms.

Most of the conspiracy theories surrounding the Sutherland Church shooting have been spread on far-right platforms (such as 4chan) and fake news websites (Selk & Grant, 2017). Kelly was alleged to be a supporter of liberal senators Hillary Clinton or Bernie Sanders (Griffin, 2017), some claimed he was a radical Muslim (Ansari, 2017), and still others proposed that he came into the church with the flag of Antifa (a radical anti-fascist group), claiming that he was part of a communist revolution (Gillin, 2017). Sadly, some conspiracy theorists staked out the hospital caring for victims of the shooting, falsely claimed that no one died and that it was a "false flag" operation (carried out by state agents, but designed to cover up their involvement), harassed the church's pastor who had lost his young daughter in the shooting, and ultimately were arrested for making terroristic threats (Flynn, 2018).

Biden–Ukraine (2017)

The Biden–Ukraine scandal has been around for a few years, but it gained even more supporters during the 2020 presidential election in the United States. Hired by the Ukrainian company of Burisma Holdings in April of 2014, Hunter Biden was employed in a high-salary position to engage in general consulting, rather than anything specific about the energy industry (Ivanova, 2019). Kranish and Stern (2019) pointed out a number of potential problems with this appointment and its suggestion of favoritism, especially because Hunter Biden's father was Vice President Joe Biden.

While no evidence of influence-peddling was unearthed (Isachenkov, 2019), these allegations came back to haunt two US presidents in the post-Obama years. For example, then President Trump made a phone call in the summer of the election year 2020 to the recently elected Ukrainian President Zelenskyy, apparently to put pressure on him to dig up dirt on Hunter Biden's dealings with Burisma, in return for receiving congressionally mandated aid to Ukraine (Sheth, 2022). Although seen by many as an effort by Trump to influence the 2020 US presidential election (Chalfant, 2020), Trump's resulting impeachment trial did not remove him from office. Also, investigations by the Homeland Security and Finance Committees determined that, while Hunter Biden had relied on his father's name (as vice president under Obama) to promote his own financial success, Joe Biden had not been responsible for arranging his son's job with Burisma (Fandos, 2020).

Even though both Donald Trump and Joe Biden were exonerated (to an extent) from wrong-doing in these events, conspiracy theorists still enthusiastically speculate about Hunter Biden and his mysterious missing laptop. For example, Donald Trump's lawyer Rudy Giuliani claimed to find a laptop left at a repair shop and published its contents (Olding, 2020). By 2021, the general consensus was that although the laptop did belong to Hunter Biden, and it did contain information about his drug use and possibly a nude photo, it did not contain any mysterious emails or indication of nefarious doings in Ukraine (Drobnic Holan, Kertscher, & Sherman, 2021).

Radio Frequency Identification Chips (2017)

Many of us want to make sure that our pets can be returned to us if they should get lost or escape. Animals implanted with passive integrated transponder (PIT) tags may include domestic pets as well as livestock such as cattle, sheep, and goats (National Livestock Identification System, 2013). These microchips have also been used by some exclusive clubs to identify their VIPs, who in turn may use them rather like a credit card "chip" to pay for services without ruining the fit of their couture with wallets or purses ("Barcelona Clubbers Get Chipped," 2004). Even hospitals, libraries, museums, and pigeon racers have used radio frequency identification chips (RFICs) in recent years.

However, and probably not surprisingly, conspiracy theories have popped up around the use of these inserted microchips. Some concerns are legitimate, of course, such as risks of skimming the chip's codes for unauthorized use, eavesdropping and invasion of privacy, and even the possibility of tumors developing at the injection site (Albrecht, 2010; Hancke, 2011). However, some bizarre theories have also cropped up surrounding RFICs, as ranked from least to most severe in an article by John Austin at www.express.co.uk (2016). For example, one conspiracy theory claims that governments will move to phase out cash so that everyone will need to be "chipped," with their real goal being monitoring their citizens. Other theories claim that these chips will be secretly implanted into us through vaccines (as discussed below in the COVID-19 section on conspiracies). The most "out there" conspiracy theory described by Austin (2016) claims that RFICs will serve as the "mark of the Beast" in a plot by the Illuminati or New World Order to control people and align them with the Antichrist.

New England Patriots (2017)

Love them or hate them, perhaps most people know something about the New England Patriots and the infamous "Deflate-Gate" scandal in which an *ESPN* reporter said that a ball attendant for the Patriots tried to introduce into the game a nonapproved and easier-to-handle football (Naqi, 2015). Star quarterback Tom Brady ended up with a four-game suspension, and he was excluded from contact with his teammates during that time.

While this scandal did not totally derail the popularity of the Patriots, it may have opened them to being targets of other conspiracy theories. For example, immediately before Super Bowl LII (in which the Patriots lost to the Philadelphia Eagles), a theory circulated on social media that the American Football Conference (AFC) championship game, in which the Patriots beat the Jacksonville Jaguars at the last minute by only four points to win the Super Bowl slot, was compromised. To conspiracists, the "evidence" that the officials threw the game included that one of the referees congratulated Tom Brady immediately after the game, that the Patriots received only one penalty during the game while the Jaguars received six penalties, and that only one other time in playoff history did a team receive only one penalty and it was again the New England Patriots in the 2011 AFC championships ("New Conspiracy Theories Embroil the New England Patriots," 2018).

Muhammadu Buhan (2017)

Muhammadu Buhan has been president of Nigeria since 2015. His public life has been full of controversy and scandals including allegations of fraud (Uko, 2003), mysterious suitcases (Aziken, 2011), and plagiarism of a Barack Obama speech from 2008 (*The Guardian*, 2016). After he took a trip to London for medical reasons in 2017, rumors began to spread that Buhan had died and been replaced by a clone named Jubril, a conspiracy theory spread by his political opposition party, the Indigenous People of Biafra (Davies, 2018). Buhan has, of course, denied the rumors.

Melania Trump (2017)

Beginning in 2017, rumors began to circulate that then First Lady Melania Trump had been replaced by a body-double (Hyde, 2017) This theory gained traction after the legs of the First Lady were missing from the public eye for five weeks after kidney surgery (Singman, 2018). While President Donald Trump has refuted these rumors, his former director of communications, Anthony Scaramucci, claims that "there is a body-double, and her sister sometimes replaces her on the campaign trail," noting that she can be identified when "Melania" behaves more affectionately with Trump (Tarbert, 2020).

Chris Cornell and Chester Bennington (2017)

Chris Cornell was a singer from the 1990s band Soundgarden, and Chester Bennington was a singer from the 1990s–2000s band Linkin Park. Both died by hanging within two months of each other, and both deaths were ruled as a suicide, but it was not long before conspiracy theories started. The theories suggest that the two men, who were close friends, were killed because they were planning to expose a pedophile ring, specifically the "Pizzagate" pedophile ring (described later). Supporters of this conspiracy theory claim that Bennington's real father was John Podesta, former White House chief of staff to President Clinton and White House counsel to President Obama, putting the two younger men close to the supposed nefarious "action" (Spollen, 2017).

Pizzagate (2017)

Although widely debunked, the "Pizzagate conspiracy theory" claimed that emails hacked from the account of John Podesta, aide to Presidents Clinton and Obama, contained secret messages linking a number of high-level Democrats and US restaurants with child sex rings (LaCapria, 2016). The frenzy surrounding this alleged sex ring conspiracy reached an apex with not only death threats directed at the owner of Comet Ping Pong restaurant in Washington, DC, but with one follower of the social media outlets that propagated this rumor (4chan, 8chan, Twitter) making the drive from North Carolina to fire shots and search for abducted children in the basement of this basement-less restaurant (Kang, 2016; Kang & Goldman, 2016).

The Pizzagate conspiracy theory was spread by many high-profile individuals including the far-right radio host Alex Jones, the YouTube personality Mike Cernovich, and the Twitter personality Jack Posobiec (Fisher, Cox,

& Hermann, 2016; Peck, 2016). Australian basketball player Andrew Bogut also supported the theory, with some claiming his knee injury was caused by nefarious persons in retaliation for his support of Pizzagate (Knoblauch, 2016). The *Daily Beast* reported that the creator of the massively popular video game *Minecraft* incorporated Pizzagate into some hybrid theory about child sex rings, holistic medicine, and a faux race war (Byrne, 2017). The Pizzagate story was also spread by the Turkish press and via tweets originating in Vietnam, Cyprus, the Czech Republic, and other foreign countries (Fisher et al., 2016; Sozeri, 2016). Pizzagate is of particular importance in the study of conspiracy theories because it appears to have been the genesis of QAnon, with its bizarre beliefs in global elites who practice sexual abuse of children, drinking their blood in Satanic rituals to keep themselves young (Hitt, 2020; "QAnon: A Glossary," 2021).

Jeffrey Epstein's Death (2019)

Jeffrey Epstein was an American financier who was arrested in 2019 on multiple sex offense charges, including sex trafficking. Denied bail, he remained in prison until his death by apparent suicide in early August of 2019. However, some conspiracists have questioned the ruling that his death was suicide, wondering how Epstein could have successfully hung himself from a bottom bunk in his prison cell ("*60 Minutes* Investigates the Death of Jeffrey Epstein," 2020). Suspicion about Epstein's death gained momentum after his defense attorney expressed his doubts that it was a suicide (Mangan and Brueninger, 2019), and conspiracy theories on Twitter accused the Clintons of having Epstein murdered as one of their "Clinton body count" of murdered enemies (Timm & Johnstone, 2019). Perhaps due to the sleazy nature of Epstein's crimes, comedians and meme-makers have had a field day with the phrase "Epstein didn't kill himself," with this phrase even interjected into the televised Golden Globe Awards and *Saturday Night Live* (Valby, 2020).

Sushant Singh Rajput (2020)

Sushant Singh Rajput was a popular Bollywood actor in India, who was found hanging from a ceiling fan at his home. Authorities ruled his death a suicide (Arora, 2020), but conspiracy theories surround his death, including that Bollywood's nepotism destroyed Rajput's mental health, or that he was murdered by a cabal of Indian politicians and Bollywood power players, or that he live-streamed his death and sold it for bitcoin on the dark web (Ananth, 2020; "Sushant Singh Rajput's Fault Is That He Believed Those Who Called Him Worthless," 2020). Believers in these conspiracy theories have an almost cultlike status, with private internet groups requiring oath-taking by new members (Ananth, 2020).

Robb Elementary School Shooting (2022)

Unfortunately, although perhaps not surprisingly, yet another school massacre occurred between the first and final drafts of this book, this time in Ulvade, Texas. An eighteen-year-old US citizen was the gunman who entered an elementary school and killed nineteen fourth graders and two teachers. In the wake of this tragedy, one would expect an outpouring of grief from all sectors of society, but this was not the case. Before even one child was buried, the conspiracy theorists were at it again. For example, according to AP News, rumors were being spread on the internet that the gunman was an illegal immigrant, or that the gunman was transgender (Klepper & Swenson, 2022). According to NPR, the attack was a false flag operation organized by the US government used to push through liberal gun control bills, or to distract from other unsavory governmental news (Yousef, 2022).

Conspiracy Beliefs about the COVID-19 Pandemic

Originating in Wuhan, China, late in 2019, the first COVID-19-related death was recorded in China on January 9, 2020 ("Coronavirus Death Toll Climbs in China, and a Lockdown Widens," 2020). The disease spread rapidly, upending economies and societies throughout the world. As of April 4, 2022, there were over six million deaths worldwide attributed to the virus (COVID-19 Dashboard by the Center for Systems Science and Engineering at Johns Hopkins University, n.d.). COVID misinformation started almost as soon as the disease was recognized. Unlike earlier conspiracy theories, many countries moved to criminalize the dissemination of COVID-19 misinformation or conspiracy theories (Pomeranz & Schwid, 2021).

Before the COVID-19 pandemic really gained hold, *The Guardian* (Taylor, 2020) addressed the spread of misinformation about the virus, such as the idea that the virus was intentionally started, that it was an escaped or leaked biological weapon, or that China's version of an energy drink or fortune cookies spread it. One of the more bizarre conspiracy theories was that the new 5G communication technology was responsible. Some of these theories had the potential to create dangerous situations, such as an Australian warning to its citizens to avoid suburbs with high concentrations of residents of Chinese descent. Also, people opposed to medical interventions to control the virus suggested drinking salt water or oregano oil, or taking vitamin C. Another so-called COVID-19 remedy, popularized by both QAnon and then President Trump, was drinking bleach.

As the pandemic lingered, the conspiracy theories multiplied, with governments getting into the act, blaming each other for the spread of the virus. For example, one idea was that COVID-19 was created by the CIA as a tool for subjugating China ("China's Rulers See the Coronavirus as a Chance to Tighten Their Grip," 2020), or that the United States created the virus at Fort Detrick and unleashed it at the 2019 Military World Games, which were, coincidentally, held in Wuhan (Houston, 2020). Russian social media was also accused of spreading the theory that the CIA created the virus and used it to target China ("Arab Writers: The Coronavirus Is Part of Biological Warfare Waged by U.S. against China," 2020). Some Arabic countries also disseminated information linking the CIA to the virus as a weapon against China, and unofficially at least, both Iran and Iraq placed responsibility for the virus on Donald Trump ("Iran Cleric Blames Trump for Coronavirus Outbreak in Religious City," 2020; Whiskeyman & Berger, 2021). Other virus conspiracy theories displayed prejudice toward religious and cultural groups, such as Jews being blamed for the pandemic in some Arabic countries as well as in Britain, Germany, and the United States ("Arab Media Accuse US, Israel of Coronavirus Conspiracy against China," 2020; Baur, 2021; Mahmood, 2020). In India, the Muslims were blamed (Datta, 2020).

Many conspiracy theories claim that the number of COVID-19 cases and deaths are either under-reported or over-reported. For example, China was accused of under-reporting case numbers early in the pandemic (Sherwell, 2020), with a video of an alleged nurse claiming far greater infection rates than those reported by the Chinese government ("China Coronavirus: Misinformation Spreads Online about Origin and Scale," 2020), with claims of mass cremations in Wuhan, supposedly to hide the true death count (Kasprak, 2020), and with decreases in cellphone subscriptions, most likely due to economic and social shutdowns, given as "proof" that millions of Chinese subscribers had died (Lajka, 2020). In the United States, conspiracy theories proposing both under-reporting and over-reporting have also been widely circulated. For example, then President Trump retweeted that COVID-19 deaths in the United States were over-counted, claiming that only 6 percent of the US deaths at that time were COVID-related (Aronczyk, 2021). Such figures can be misleading because not all death certificates gave COVID-19 as the *only* cause of death, with many deaths at this time due to comorbid conditions that were coexistent with or exacerbated by the COVID virus (Spencer, 2020). In addition, privacy laws and inconsistent reporting across state jurisdictions have led to under-reporting of COVID-related deaths (Piller, 2020).

Some of the more bizarre COVID-19 conspiracy theories center on preventions and cures. At the very start of the pandemic in the United States, Norwegian Cruise Line advertised that the virus could not survive in warm climates, encouraging potential passengers to book a trip to the Caribbean to avoid getting sick (Cardona, 2020). Given that the virus was sometimes found in semen, some researchers initially claimed the virus might be sexually transmitted ("COVID-19 Found in Semen of Infected Men, Say Chinese Doctors," 2020). Changing ideas about COVID prevention practices led to some potentially dangerous recommendations. Wearing face masks was one of the earliest suggested prevention measures, but with shifting recommendations given by the US Surgeon General (Madhani, 2020), and President Duterte of the Philippines recommending cleaning masks with gasoline if other disinfectants were not available ("Rodrigo Duterte: 'I'm Not Joking— Clean Masks with Petrol,'" 2020). Social media suggested alcohol consumption stopped the virus, which had fatal consequences in Muslim countries, where drinking ethanol alcohol was prohibited so some individuals consumed the deadly methanol alcohol instead. Iranian social media also circulated reports that whiskey and honey cured COVID, with deleterious results for people's health (Jolly, 2020; Trew, 2020). Other substances, both legal and illegal, were also proposed to offer COVID-19 protection. Tobacco smoking increased in France after a hospital found that smoking and COVID infections were negatively associated for their patients (van Zyl-Smit, Richards, & Leone, 2020). Twitter in both Europe and Africa claimed that cocaine would sterilize the nostrils, preventing COVID infection (Crellin, 2020). In India, TikTok recommended that people eat cabbage as well as the fruit of the datura plant, part of the nightshade family ("WHO Did Not Warn Against Eating Cabbage during the COVID-19 Pandemic," 2020; "Twelve Taken Ill after Consuming 'Coronavirus Shaped' Datura Seeds," 2020).

Once the vaccines were developed and approved for use among at least a subsection of adults, conspiracy theories and misinformation pivoted away from the causes of the virus and questionable preventative measures, and instead focused on the vaccines. These conspiracy theories were especially popular among those in the already anti-vaccination community. For example, these new conspiracy theories questioned the effectiveness of the new vaccines (Aronczyk, 2021), their side effects, and even whether they were really vaccines against COVID or something else more sinister. For example, concerns were raised that the vaccine would cause blood clots, lead to female infertility, cause cancer, or alter a person's DNA (Gregory, 2021; Kertschner, 2021).

Some of the COVID-19 vaccine conspiracy theories verge on the bizarre. For example, one African country saw Facebook posts claiming that polio vaccines distributed in their country carried the COVID-19 virus (Rauhala, Paquette, & George, 2020). The ultra-conservative news outlet Newsmax reported that the Moderna vaccine contained a tracking agent, allowing the government to monitor movements of all vaccinated persons (Evon, 2021).

NBC News reported in late fall of 2021 that some anti-vaxxers were getting vaccinated to comply with workplace mandates, then bathing in a concoction of clay, borax, and Epsom salt, which they believed would leach the vaccine from their bodies ("Vaccine Holdouts Are Caving to Mandates—Then Scrambling to Undo It," 2021). Perhaps most unusual are the theories that the vaccine injects a microchip into people that makes them interface with 5G towers (Bischoff, 2021), or that the vaccine makes a person's body magnetized (Camero, 2021).

Conspiracy Beliefs about the 2020 US Presidential Election

As if the United States and the world were not disrupted enough by COVID-19, the US presidential election of 2020 and the certification of the election in 2021 whipped conspiracy theorists into a frenzy. Even before the election, allegations of voter fraud were vociferously and publicly voiced, primarily by Trump and pro-Trump Republicans (Corasaniti, Epstein, & Rutenberg, 2020). During the election, conspiracists were concerned that malfeasance was behind the delayed announcement of the winner by a few days, probably because of the unusually high number of mail-in votes due to the pandemic lockdowns (Saul & Hakim, 2020). After the election, lawyers for the Trump administration filed numerous lawsuits alleging fraud, none of which were successful at being heard in court (Pengelly, 2020). These attempts to change the outcome of the election culminated in the "Stop the Steal" campaign, with the January 6, 2021, attack on the US Capitol to prevent the certification of the election (Solnit, 2021; Triomphe, 2020). Cohen (2021) has identified six conspiracy theories about this election, all of which may have contributed to the January 6 insurrection: (1) theories claiming that the Dominion voting machines flipped or deleted Trump votes; (2) theories claiming that the ballots of Maricopa County, Arizona, were compromised with Sharpie markers; (3) theories claiming that mail-in votes were fraudulent; (4) theories claiming that bags of Trump ballots were discarded; (5) theories claiming that Trump poll watchers were prevented from observing the fairness of elections; and (6) theories claiming that thousands of dead people voted and/or that people voted multiple times. It is worth looking at some of these theories separately.

Dominion Voting Systems has designed and produced electronic voting machines, distributing them primarily in the United States and Canada ("Company Overview of Dominion Voting Systems Corporation," 2017). Following the 2020 election, Trump and his surrogates began propagating the rumor that Dominion voting machines literally changed Trump votes to Biden votes (Nicas, 2020). This story was fueled by a tweet by Trump's press secretary, Kayleigh McEnany, stating that 6,000 expected Republican ballots in Antrim County, Michigan, were logged in as Democrat, suggesting that other counties in the state experienced a similar issue (McEnany, 2020). In fairness, Antrim County did mistakenly report Biden as the winner in their county early on election night, but election officials quickly spotted the error and corrected it (McNamara, 2020). Also, Trump's attorney Sidney Powell sued the state of Georgia, claiming fraud and demanding that the results be dismissed after their electoral votes went to Biden (Watson, 2020). This theory of fraudulent votes continued to snowball, with one QAnon misinformation spreader falsely claiming that the user manuals for Dominion voting machines gave instructions on how to change votes that were already cast (Harwell, 2020).

Somewhat related to the Dominion Voting machine conspiracy theories was "SharpieGate." This theory focused primarily on the state of Arizona, and later Pennsylvania, with conspiracists claiming that Sharpie pens would invalidate a person's vote, and that *only* Trump supporters were given Sharpies to mark their ballots (Schulberg, 2020). The reality? Sharpies were actually recommended by the Dominion Voting machine manufacturer because Sharpies would not smudge while being counted and therefore would actually give a much more accurate count of votes (Cohen, 2021; Maricopa County Elections Department, 2020). These theories remain popular with Trump and some of his supporters, even those in Congress (Cooper, 2021).

Mail-in voting became very popular in the 2020 election cycle, partly due to COVID-19 lockdown conditions, but with roughly 75 percent of mail-in ballots cast being from Democrats ("The 2020 Voting Experience: Coronavirus, Mail Concerns Factored into Deciding How to Vote," 2020). Even prior to the election, Trump stated, loudly and vociferously, that mail-in voting was rife with fraud (Quinn, 2020a). However, mail-in voting has been an option since the Civil War (Cohen, 2021), and cybersecurity experts have documented its safety (Patterson, 2020).

Viral videos circulated immediately after the election spread other conspiracy theories that ballots had been mishandled, discarded, or stolen (Lewis, 2020). For example, one video purportedly showed a poll worker throwing out a ballot, when he was actually throwing out a piece of scrap paper, but nevertheless, this poll worker was later physically threatened by Trump supporters (Connelly, 2020). Other videos presented by election conspiracists in support of the idea that the election was "stolen" included a cameraman in Detroit supposedly loading up ballots to carry them away from a polling place, when he was actually just loading up his camera equipment, and two mail bags found by a road in Washington state that included unopened, and hence, unmarked ballots (Cohen, 2020). Another complaint made by election conspiracists was that Trump "poll watchers" were not allowed to get as close to the election action as they were permitted by law, which is six feet (Quinn, 2020b). As Pennsylvania was a hotly contested state, there was much to be gained from challenging its election results, and this conspiracy belief may have begun in Philadelphia, where unofficial poll watchers were banned from rooms where votes are counted (which is the law), making this belief based more on a misunderstanding of election laws rather than an active attempt to overthrow the election (Cohen, 2020).

Finally, Trump himself claimed that "massive numbers of dead people voted in the 2020 Presidential election" (Manjarres, 2021). Fox News commentator and avid Trump supporter Tucker Carlson (2020) pointed the blame squarely on the Democrats, claiming that approximately one-eighth of voter registrations were invalid due to death or other circumstances. Democrats may have inadvertently encouraged the idea of fraudulent voters with their support of various bills to increase the scope of mail-in balloting, although it is unclear why dead people *only* vote for Democrats. In truth, there are some cases of dead people who have legitimately voted, such as when they send them in before they die (Farley, 2020), but only one case was documented of someone casting a vote for a deceased person (Cohen, 2020); a man in Pennsylvania registered his dead mother to vote, then cast her vote for *Donald Trump*. Although Trump himself encouraged his supporters to try to vote twice (Cohen, 2020), even the conservative Heritage Foundation found no evidence of widespread voting fraud in 2020, only identifying seventeen cases throughout the nation.

CONCLUSION

The past twenty years have seen a clear proliferation of conspiracy theories, both those that appear silly and harmless, and those with dangerous outcomes for individuals and society. Many of the more frivolous conspiracy theories (such as celebrity doppelgangers) seem to have started as a joke or hoax, but many of the more serious and consequential theories have appeared to take root during times of social upheaval both historically and in contemporary times. For example, conspiracy theories surrounding the death and resurrection of the Roman Empower Nero occurred at a time of great social change as Christianity began to spread through the Roman world. Similarly, stories of the Illuminati as a secret society germinated in the late 1700s, a time in which the Western world was characterized by exploration and revolution. No one can argue that the 1960s in the United States was not also a time of great social change, with the Kennedy assassination, with advances of the space program, with social movements for civil rights, gay rights, and women's rights, and with escalation of the Cold War and tensions with the Soviet Union. In the new millennium, we have also experienced the 9/11 attacks, the first Black president of the United States, another hotly contested presidential election in 2020, and a global pandemic. All this social upheaval undoubtedly can lead to social feelings of ennui and anomie, leaving individuals feeling confused, alone, and powerless. Combined with the increasing influence of the internet as the fastest (and possibly most abused) source of information the world has ever known, it is no surprise that so many people adopt conspiracy theories that, in the past, would have been relegated to the dustbin of history.

Chapter 5

The Present Study

PURPOSE OF PRESENT STUDY

The director of the FBI has reported that the present greatest threat to national security in the United States is from home-grown terrorists (Solman et al., 2021) such as the conspiracy believers who attacked the Capitol on January 6, 2021. It has now become urgent that new research be conducted not only to examine a broader range of demographic characteristics associated with adoption of conspiracy theories and violent ideation (*WHO?*), but also to understand the sequence of psychological events that may lead individuals to these potentially destructive beliefs (*WHY?*). The present study aims to fill these research gaps. More specifically, to examine *WHO?* is at greatest risk for adopting extreme beliefs, we examine thirteen demographic characteristics (age, gender, racial identity, Hispanic ethnicity, education, employment status, income, military experience, household size, intimate partner status, social media hours, rural/urban environment, and political affiliation) for their association with five general types of conspiracy beliefs (government malfeasance, malevolent world powers, extraterrestrial coverup, personal well-being threats, control of information) as well as violent ideation. To examine psychologically *WHY?* individuals might adopt these extreme beliefs, we evaluate a three-step sequence suggested by the threat appraisal and coping theory (Lazarus and Folkman 1984): *life stressors → powerlessness as PTSD → extreme beliefs*. In this sequence, we believe that when individuals perceive intense life stressors (such as health, money, loneliness problems), and when they also experience a sense of powerlessness (displayed as PTSD symptoms of sleep disturbance, memory lapses, hypervigilance, social withdrawal), they are at increased risk for adopting extreme beliefs as "cognitive coping mechanisms" that may enhance their sense of understanding, strength, and unity with others who hold similar views. Results from these analyses of *WHO?*

59

tends to adopt extreme beliefs and psychologically *WHY?* they do so could guide future prevention and intervention efforts by concerned families, therapists, and governments to target anti-conspiracy messages more effectively for individuals at greatest risk. Study results could also help focus prevention efforts on reducing specific life stressors (health, money, loneliness), and/or reducing symptoms of powerlessness (PTSD) that serve as pathways toward dangerous conspiracy beliefs.

THE ROLE OF VIOLENT IDEATION

Angry thoughts of violence to defend oneself and right wrongs may have a special role as a cognitive coping response to life stressors combined with powerlessness (Misiak, Samochowiec, Bhui, Schouler-Ocak, Demunter, Kucy, Raballo, Gorwood, Frydecka, & Dom, 2019). Past research suggests that when individuals begin to have angry thoughts, they immediately feel energized, strong, and blameless (Herrero, Gadea, Rodríquez-Alarcón, Espert, & Salvador, 2010; Kazén, Kuenne, Frankenberg, & Quirin, 2012), all of which could alleviate their sense of powerlessness. We anticipated that besides conspiracy beliefs, violent ideation would be another *extreme belief* that would be associated with the experience of life stressors combined with powerlessness.

NEW FEATURES OF PRESENT STUDY

One new feature of the present study is that it expands the question of *WHO?* is most likely to adopt extreme beliefs, with our study evaluating thirteen demographic characteristics for their association with conspiracy beliefs and violent ideation. The present study also expands the question of *WHY?* individuals adopt extreme beliefs, with consideration of the role of three life stressors (health, money, loneliness), and with consideration of the role of PTSD symptoms. More specifically, using threat appraisal and coping theory (Lazarus & Folkman, 1984) as our guide, the present study is the first *theoretical* examination of a three-step psychological sequence: *life stressors → powerlessness as PTSD → extreme beliefs.* Another new feature of the present study is that it evaluates five types of conspiracy beliefs as its outcome measures: government malfeasance, malevolent world power, extraterrestrial coverup, personal well-being threats, and control of information. Finally, the present study adds violent ideation as another form of extreme belief, in which individuals express willingness to use physical violence when threatened or their rights are violated.

If support is found for the patterns of life stressors, PTSD, conspiracy beliefs, and violent ideation evaluated in the present study, perhaps it will help to explain (but not defend) some of the thoughts driving individuals who violently attacked the US Capitol on January 6, 2021, as well as those involved in other instances of violent activism. Another benefit of the present study's examination of three *specific* life stressors, the five types of conspiracy beliefs, and the *specific* symptoms of PTSD as a mediator between them is that, if found significant, these characteristics can all become the focus of interventions to alleviate the suffering they bring to individuals, and to reduce the risk for violent actions driven by them.

HYPOTHESES

In our examinations of *WHO?* adopts extreme beliefs, past research suggested that younger age, no college education, low income, and conservative political leanings would be significant predictors of conspiracy beliefs (Abraham, Adorjan, Ahmed, Auwal, Bjedov, & Bobes, 2022; Andrade, 2021; Carey, 2019; Crocker, Luhtanen, Broadnax, & Blaine, 1999; Davis, Wetherell, & Henry, 2018; Hettich, Beutel, Ernst, Schliessler, Kampling, Kruse, & Braehler, 2022; Klonoff & Landrine, 1999; Prichard & Christman, 2020; Radnitz & Underwood, 2017; Romer & Jamieson, 2020; Stroope, Kroeger, Williams, & Baker, 2021; Swami, 2012; van Prooijen, 2016). In our examinations of *WHY?* individuals adopt extreme beliefs, principles of the threat appraisal and coping theory (Lazarus & Folkman, 1984) led us to the hypothesis that some or all of the three life stressors we considered (health problems, money problems, social loneliness problems) would be linked, via the powerlessness of PTSD symptoms, with some or all of the six extreme beliefs we evaluated (five general conspiracy beliefs, violent ideation). Originally, we believed that the social stressor of loneliness would be the most significant life stressor in the proposed three-step sequence (*life stressors → powerlessness as PTSD → extreme beliefs*) because of its prominence in past research as a predictor for other troublesome coping behaviors such as violence in prisoners (Camlibel, Can, & Hendy, 2021), and hoarding, disordered eating, and opioid abuse in nationwide samples of US citizens (Black & Hendy, 2018; Hendy, Black, Can, Fleischut, & Aksen, 2018).

However, our survey was launched in the United States during the first week of March of 2022, in the context of a number of high-impact and even historic events, all of which could have worsened health, money, and loneliness stressors of US citizens:

1. The COVID-19 pandemic was trending downward, but new variants of the virus continued to emerge. It had overwhelmed hospitals and health care providers, resulting in over 900,000 deaths, with "long-haul" symptoms in many of its survivors. It had required social lockdowns that separated families and friends from each other, workers from their workplaces, and travelers from their destinations (Liebowitz, 2021).
2. An eighty-year record-breaking inflation was occurring, along with poor stock market performance, as well as supply-chain disasters of cargo containers stuck outside port cities (Ivanov & Dolgui, 2020).
3. News outlets offered daily displays of protracted hostilities between individuals at different ends of the liberal-to-conservative political spectrum, especially concerning the 2020 presidential election results (Landry, Ihm, Kwit, & Schooler, 2021).
4. News outlets also covered dramatic incidents of police officers killing unarmed Black citizens, citizens attacking police officers, mass shootings including at schools, and hate crimes based on race, religion, or national origin (West, Greenland, & Laar, 2021).
5. The Russian invasion of Ukraine reignited international "battle lines," threatened World War III scenarios, and meanwhile resulted in additional inflation hardships for US citizens (Payne et al., 2022).

Because of these varied and widespread threats to US citizens, and the sense of powerlessness we believed they would produce, we changed our hypothesis to include all three stressors (health, money, loneliness) as probable predictors of conspiracy beliefs and violent ideation, which we believe serve as "cognitive coping mechanisms" to make the person feel smarter, stronger, and more united with like-minded others.

PART 3

Research Methodology

Chapter 6

Study Participants

Study participants included 977 US adults eighteen years or older recruited to complete an anonymous survey on "life stressors and belief systems" through paid survey services, with Qualtrics used to prepare the survey, and with Prolific used to distribute the survey nationwide for a sample of 1,000 US citizens as representative as possible to US Census data. While these paid survey services attempt to match sample demographics to national demographics, some research suggests they produce samples that are somewhat older, more often White in reported racial identity, more urban, more educated, with higher incomes (Heen, Lieverman, & Miethe, 2014). However, in a recent comparison of online survey services, researchers concluded in their abstract that "only Prolific provided high data quality" (Eyal, David, Andrew, Zak, & Ekaterina, 2021).

For the present sample, 1,000 US adults were sent our survey, and 977 returned them, for a response rate of 97.7 percent. The mean age of respondents was 45.08 years, 48.5 percent were male and 50.0 percent were female, 77.9 percent reported their racial identity as White and 12.3 percent reported it as Black, 6.9 percent reported their ethnic identity as Latino, 55.7 percent had completed a four-year college degree, 48.6 percent of them had full-time employment, their mean yearly income was $66,673 before taxes, 6.3 percent had military experience, their mean social media exposure was 1.75 hours/day, 50.3 percent had a romantic partner or spouse, 25.1 percent lived in large urban cities, and their mean rating for their liberal to conservative political views (from one to seven) was 3.24. Table 6.1 shows additional details about participant demographics, calculated using SPSS 28 software.

Table 6.1. Descriptive Statistics for Participant Demographics (*n* = 977)

Variable	%
Gender identity	
Male	48.5
Female	51.0
Other	1.0
Latino ethnic identity	6.9
College degree (four-year)	55.7
Full-time employment	48.6
Has partner/spouse	50.3
Has military experience	6.3
Racial identity	
White	77.9
Black	12.3
Asian	5.7
Other	4.1
Regional environment	
Large urban city	25.1
Medium-size city	41.4
Small town	23.8
Rural	9.7

Variable	Mean	SD	Range
Age (years)	45.08	16.15	18–92
Yearly income	$66,673	$32,908	<$10,000–$110,000+
Household others	1.42	1.05	0–3+
Social media (hours/day)	1.75	.89	0–3+
Conservatism (7-point rating)	3.24	1.74	1–7

Chapter 7

Survey Procedures

The anonymous survey was described to participants as a study of how "life stressors were associated with beliefs of US citizens." The survey asked participants to report thirteen demographic characteristics and ten study variables. Table 7.1 shows descriptive statistics for the study variables, calculated with SPSS 28 software. The participant demographics were summarized in table 6.1 and included:

Table 7.1. Descriptive Statistics for Study Variables ($n = 977$)

Variable	Cronbach's α	Mean	SD	Range
Life stressors				
Health stressors	—	2.81	1.00	1–5
Money stressors	.85	1.46	.75	1–5
Loneliness stressors	.94	2.33	1.07	1–5
PTSD symptoms (powerlessness)	.82	2.48	.77	1–5
Extreme beliefs				
Government malfeasance	.91	2.40	1.25	1–5
Malevolent world power	.93	2.23	1.23	1–5
Extraterrestrial coverup	.88	1.98	1.11	1–5
Personal well-being threat	.86	2.07	1.09	1–5
Control of information	.80	2.74	1.14	1–5
Violent ideation	.83	1.77	.79	1–5

1. *Age*—It was asked as years of age at last birthday.
2. *Gender identity*—It was asked as male, female, or other, then collapsed to male, female.
3. *Racial identity*—It was asked as White, Black, Asian, or other.
4. *Latino ethnic identity*—It was asked as yes or no.
5. *College education*—It was asked as no high school degree, high school, some college or technical training, four-year college degree, master's

degree, or doctoral degree, then collapsed to at least college degree, yes or no.

6. *Full-time employment*—It was asked as unemployed, retired, part-time, or full-time, then collapsed to full-time, yes or no.

7. *Yearly income*—It was asked as yearly income before taxes in $10,000 increments from $10,000 to $110,000+.

8. *Partner status*—It was asked as single, separated, divorced, widowed, have partner but live apart, live with partner, or live with spouse, then collapsed to partner/spouse, yes or no.

9. *Household others*—It was asked as the number of others living in the present household.

10. *Social media exposure*—It was asked as usual daily time spent on social media (Facebook, Twitter, Snapchat, Instagram, etc.) from zero to three-plus hours per day.

11. *Military experience*—It was asked as none, yes but not combat, or yes with combat, then collapsed to military experience, yes or no.

12. *Regional environment*—It was asked as large urban city, medium-size city, small town, or rural.

13. *Conservative political affiliation*—It was asked as a seven-point rating from 1 = extremely liberal, 2 = very liberal, 3 = slightly liberal, 4 = moderate, 5 = slightly conservative, 6 = very conservative, 7 = extremely conservative.

The survey also asked participants to respond to brief measures of our ten study variables that included three life stressors (health, money, loneliness), powerlessness (displayed as PTSD symptoms), five conspiracy beliefs (government malfeasance, malevolent world power, extraterrestrial coverup, threats to personal well-being, control of information), and violent ideation (expressed as reported willingness to commit violence when threatened). To keep the survey brief while using measures likely to be psychometrically sound, most study variables were evaluated with items selected from published, psychometrically tested scales. To further reduce respondent burden and obtain as large a response rate as possible, we used a consistent five-point rating throughout the survey for these measures of study variables (1 = never, 2 = rarely, 3 = sometimes, 4 = often, 5 = always), asking participants to report how often they had experienced each situation within the past year to focus their response in time.

Chapter 8

Measurement of Study Variables

The ten study variables (three life stressors, powerlessness, five conspiracy beliefs, violent ideation) were measured using from one to seven items, for which participants were asked to provide ratings of how much the description applied to them during the past year. The score for each study variable was then calculated as this rating (if only one summary item was used) or as the mean of the ratings (if multiple items were used), with higher scores indicating more of the participant characteristic being measured. In addition, Cronbach's α values were calculated for each study variable measured with multiple items to assess their internal reliability.

HEALTH STRESSORS

Health stressors were measured with a single item that asked participants how often they were worried about their physical health during the past year. They were asked to respond with the five-point rating (1 = never, 2 = rarely, 3 = sometimes, 4 = often, 5 = always). This rating was used as the score for health stressors, with higher scores indicating more health stressors.

MONEY STRESSORS

Money stressors were measured with four items derived from the Financial Stress Questionnaire (http://fastrakproject.org). Participants were asked to use the five-point rating (1 = never, 2 = rarely, 3 = sometimes, 4 = often, 5 = always) to report how often they had experienced each money stressor during the past year. The score for money stressors was calculated as the mean five-point rating for these four items (see below), with higher scores indicating more money stressors (Cronbach's α = .85).

1. "Unable to pay rent, mortgage, or utility bills on time."
2. "Need to sell or pawn something to get money."
3. "Must ask for financial help from family, friends, or agencies."
4. "Miss meals because of lack of money."

LONELINESS STRESSORS

The social stress of loneliness was measured with the six-item Revised UCLA Loneliness Scale (Wongpakaran, Wongpakaran, Pinyopornpanish, Simcharoen, Suradom, Varnado, & Kuntawong, 2020). Participants were asked to use the five-point rating (1 = never, 2 = rarely, 3 = sometimes, 4 = often, 5 = always) to report how often they agreed with each description during the past year. The score for loneliness was calculated as the mean five-point rating for these six items (see below), with higher scores indicating more loneliness (Cronbach's α = .94).

1. "You lacked companionship."
2. "You felt alone."
3. "You were no longer close to anyone."
4. "You felt left out."
5. "You felt that no one really knows you well."
6. "People were around you, but not with you."

PTSD (POWERLESSNESS)

Powerlessness was measured in two ways. One measure evaluated *displayed* symptoms of powerlessness using six items from the seventeen-item Posttraumatic Diagnostic Scale (Foa, Cashman, Joycox, & Perry, 1997). This scale evaluates an individual's post-traumatic stress disorder (PTSD) symptoms of losing control over their sleep, memory, emotions, body responses, and socializing. Participants were asked to use the five-point rating (1 = never, 2 = rarely, 3 = sometimes, 4 = often, 5 = always) to report how often each experience applied to them during the past year. The score for displayed powerless (PTSD symptoms) was calculated as the mean five-point rating for these six items (see below), with higher scores indicating more displayed powerlessness with PTSD symptoms (Cronbach's α = .82).

1. "I had nightmares."
2. "I had trouble remembering things."
3. "I tried to avoid activities, places, people."

4. "I was overly alert."
5. "I was easily startled."
6. "I felt irritable."

We believed that an individual could be displaying daily symptoms of powerlessness with or without being consciously aware of a sense of powerlessness. However, as a check of whether the *displayed* PTSD symptoms of powerlessness showed convergent validity with the individual's *perceived* powerlessness, we also gathered a measure of powerlessness using four items from the Levinson Internal Locus of Control Scale (ILOC; Lao, 1978; Levenson, 1972). Participants were asked to use the five-point rating (1 = never, 2 = rarely, 3 = sometimes, 4 = often, 5 = always) to report how often they agreed with each perception during the past year. Item ratings were then reversed (1 = 5, 2 = 4, 3 = 3, 4 = 2, 5 = 1) so that the *higher* the rating, the *worse* their sense of personal control, or the more perceived powerlessness they experienced. The score for *perceived* powerlessness was calculated as the mean five-point rating for the four items, with higher scores indicating more perceived powerlessness (Cronbach's α = .79). Items on this perceived powerlessness measure included:

1. "When I make plans, I can almost certainly make them work out."
2. "I can pretty much determine what will happen in my life."
3. "When I get what I want, it is usually because I worked hard for it."
4. "My life is determined by my own actions."

The score for perceived powerlessness was found to be significantly but only moderately correlated with the PTSD score (r = .32, n = 977, p < .001), supporting the idea that individuals may have *displayed* powerlessness with symptoms of PTSD (loss of control over their sleep, memory, bodily responses, emotions, social life) without experiencing *perceived* powerlessness. We selected displayed powerlessness as our possible mediating variable between life stressors and extreme beliefs because, if found significant as such a link, it is more treatable with available targeted interventions. In contrast, general perceptions of powerlessness are less focused and, therefore, more challenging for interventions.

FIVE GENERAL CONSPIRACY BELIEFS

Five general conspiracy beliefs were measured with subscales from the complete fifteen-item Generic Conspiracist Belief Scale (GCBS; Brotherton, French, & Pickering, 2013). Rather than measure *specific* conspiracy beliefs, which can change rapidly in today's social media age (such as QAnon, Anti-Vaxx, Holocaust denial, moon landing denial, flat Earth, Stop the Steal), and which we were concerned could trigger some participant's rejection of our entire survey if they held strong views about them, we chose to measure more *general* conspiracy beliefs that would include yet transcend such fleeting specific conspiracies. The conspiracy beliefs included in the GCBS were government malfeasance, malevolent global forces, extraterrestrial coverup, threats to personal well-being, and control of information, with three items for each of these subscales. Participants were asked to use the five-point rating (1 = never, 2 = rarely, 3 = sometimes, 4 – often, 5 – always) to report how often they agreed with each opinion during the past year. The score for each conspiracy belief was calculated as the mean five-point rating for the three items in its subscale (see below), with higher scores indicating more of the conspiracy belief.

Government Malfeasance (Cronbach's $\alpha = .91$):

1. "The government is involved in murder of innocent citizens and/or well-known public figures and keeps this a secret."
2. "The government permits or perpetrates acts of terrorism on its own soil, disguising its involvement."
3. "The government uses people as patsies to hide its involvement in criminal activity."

Malevolent World Power (Cronbach's α – .93):

1. "The power held by heads of state is second to that of small unknown groups who really control world politics."
2. "A small, secret group of people is responsible for making all major world decisions, such as going to war."
3. "Certain significant events have resulted from activity of a small group who secretly manipulate world events."

Extraterrestrial Coverup (Cronbach's $\alpha = .88$):

1. "Secret organizations communicate with extraterrestrials but keep this fact from the public."
2. "Evidence of extraterrestrial contact is being concealed from the public."
3. "Some UFO sightings and rumors are planned or staged in order to distract the public from real extraterrestrial contact."

Threats to Personal Well-Being (Cronbach's $\alpha = .86$):

1. "The spread of certain viruses and/or diseases is the result of the deliberate, concealed efforts of some organization."
2. "Technology with mind-control capacities is used on people without their knowledge."
3. "Experiments with new drugs or technologies are routinely carried out on the public without their knowledge or consent."

Control of Information (Cronbach's α = .80):

1. "Groups of scientists manipulate, fabricate, or suppress evidence in order to deceive the public."
2. "New and advanced technology which would harm current industry is being suppressed."
3. "A lot of important information is deliberately concealed from the public out of self-interest."

VIOLENT IDEATION

Willingness to commit violence was measured with five items from the nine-item Physical Aggression Subscale (Buss & Perry, 1992). Participants were asked to use the five-point rating (1 = never, 2 = rarely, 3 = sometimes, 4 = often, 5 = always) to report how often each description applied to them during the past year. The score for violent ideation was calculated as the mean five-point rating for the five items (see below), with higher scores indicating more violent ideation (Cronbach's α = .83).

1. "Given enough provocation, I may hit another person."
2. "If somebody hits me, I hit back."
3. "If I must resort to violence to protect my rights, I will."
4. "There are people who pushed me so far that we came to blows."
5. "I have become so mad that I have broken things."

PRELIMINARY ANALYSES OF STUDY VARIABLES

Table 8.1 shows bivariate correlations for the above ten study variables, calculated with SPSS 28 software. Figure 8.1 shows a comparison of the mean five-point ratings given by the 977 US citizens of the present study for the three life stressors (health, money, loneliness). A repeated-measures ANOVA revealed significant differences for the intensity of the three life stressors ($F_{(2, 1952)}$ = 761.00, $p < .001$), with visual examination suggesting that present

Table 8.1. Bivariate Correlations between Study Variables ($n = 977$)

Life stressors				Extreme beliefs					
Health	Money	Lonely	PTSD	Govern	World	Aliens	Person	Inform	Violence
Health	.305*	.351*	.468*	.049	.047	.063	.049	.090	.055
Money		.377*	.390*	.256*	.224*	.222*	.244*	.220*	.194*
Lonely			.584*	.220*	.154*	.168*	.186*	.238*	.251*
PTSD				.243*	.195*	.197*	.197*	.275*	.258*
Govern					.822*	.580*	.787*	.793*	.330*
World						.631*	.822*	.751*	.311*
Aliens							.694*	.583*	.307*
Person								.760*	.316*
Inform									.303*
Violence									
*p < .001									

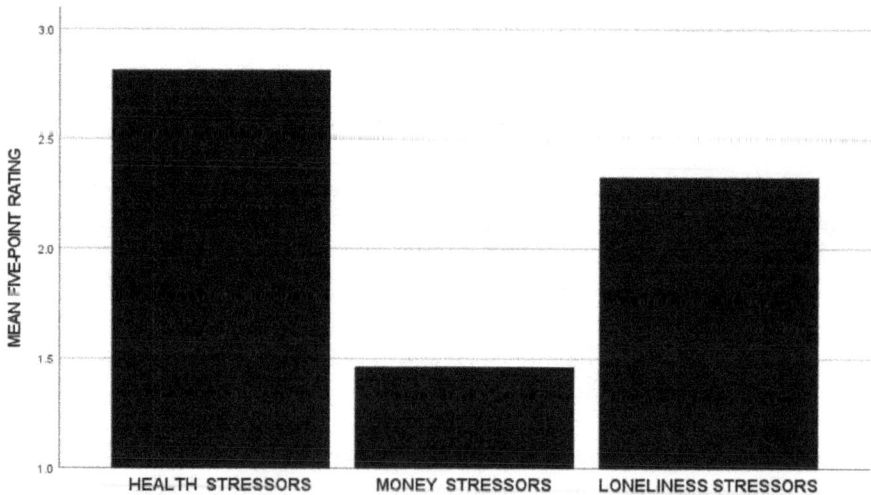

Figure 8.1. Comparison of three life stressors. *Created by the authors.*

study participants were most concerned about health and loneliness stressors, perhaps because of the COVID-19 pandemic and its social distancing require-ments they had experienced for the past two years. Additionally, a repeated-measures ANOVA revealed significant differences for the intensity of the five conspiracy beliefs ($F_{(4, 3904)} = 238.05, p < .001$), with visual examination of figure 8.2 suggesting that present study participants were most likely to hold conspiracy beliefs about control of information and government malfeasance, again perhaps because of reactions to news and policies associated with the COVID-19 pandemic.

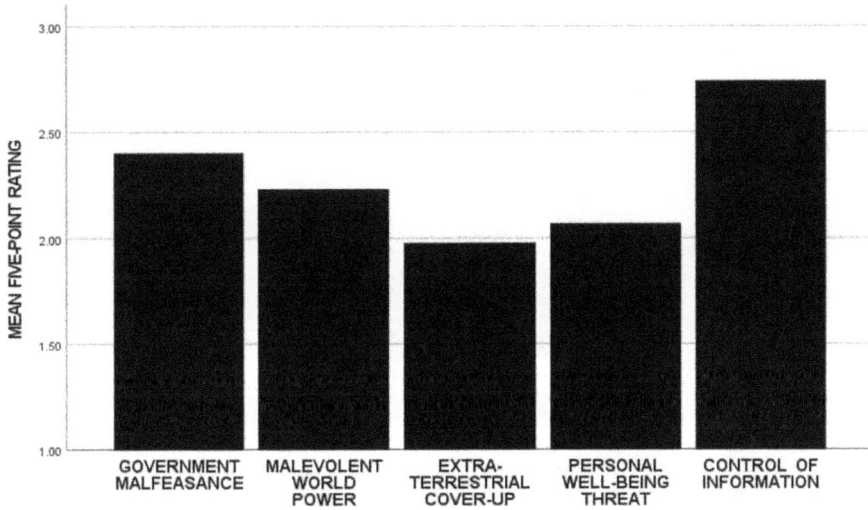

Figure 8.2. Comparison of five conspiracy beliefs. *Created by the authors.*

PART 4

Data Analysis and Results

Chapter 9

Demographics and Life Stressors

STATISTICAL ANALYSIS

Examination of how the thirteen participant demographics were associated with each of the three life stressors (health, money, loneliness) was done using SPSS 28 software to conduct multiple regression analysis, with the score for the life stressor serving as the outcome variable, and with the thirteen participant demographics serving as possible predictor variables. The advantage of such multiple regression analysis is that it evaluates each predictor's *unique* contribution to explaining the variance in the outcome variable, with the other predictors already taken into account. We believed this was especially important because some demographics may be expected to be correlated with other demographics, such as college education, income, partner status, and number of household others. Also, because of the number of analyses using the same variables, we set our criterion for significance to the conservative value of $p < .001$ to reduce the possibility of study-wise Type I errors. Variables were measured as described in chapters 7 and 8. The three life stressors included:

1. Health stressors—a numerical variable from 1.00 to 5.00
2. Money stressors—a numerical variable from 1.00 to 5.00
3. Loneliness stressors—a numerical variable from 1.00 to 5.00

The thirteen participant demographics evaluated as possible predictors for each of the three life stressors included:

1. *Age*—a numerical variable from eighteen years or more
2. *Male gender identity*—effect coded as male (1), female (0)

3. *Racial identity*—effect coded with three vectors as Black (1) versus White (0), Asian (1) versus White (0), other (1) versus White (0)
4. *Latino ethnic identity*—effect coded as yes (1), no (0)
5. *College education*—effect coded as yes (1), no (0)
6. *Full-time employment*—effect coded as yes (1), no (0)
7. *Yearly income*—a numerical variable from $10,000 to $110,000+
8. *Partner status*—effect coded as yes (1), no (0)
9. *Household others*—a numerical variable from zero to three-plus
10. *Social media exposure*—a numerical variable from zero to three-plus hours per day
11. *Military experience*—effect coded as yes (1), no (0)
12. *Regional environment*—effect coded with three vectors as medium city (1) versus urban (0), small town (1) versus urban (0), and rural (1) versus urban (0)
13. *Conservative political affiliation*—a numerical variable from one to seven

Table 9.1 shows results for the multiple regression analyses to examine how participant demographics were associated with three life stressors (health, money, loneliness). Using our conservative criterion for significance ($p < .001$), more health stressors were reported by participants with lower incomes and less conservative political affiliations. More money stressors were reported by participants with lower incomes and who lived in urban environments (as opposed to rural environments). More loneliness stressors were reported by participants with younger ages, lower incomes, and those without partners.

VISUAL EXAMINATION

To provide a more visual examination of how significant demographics in the above multiple regression analyses were associated with life stressors (health, money, loneliness), we used SPSS 28 software to prepare bar graphs showing life stressor scores across clusters of study participants. For example, because age was found associated with loneliness stressors, we prepared graphs displaying loneliness scores for five age-group clusters (or "generations") of US citizens:

1. Silent Generation—77–97 years of age ($n = 8$)
2. Baby Boomer—58–76 years of age ($n = 273$)
3. Generation X—42–57 years of age ($n = 242$)

4. Generation Y—26–41 years of age (*n* = 301)
5. Generation Z—18–25 years of age (*n* = 142)

Figure 9.1 shows the bar graph of loneliness scores for these five generations, with younger generations reporting the most loneliness.

Because yearly income was found associated with more of all three life
stressors (health, money, loneliness), we prepared graphs displaying each
stressor score for US citizens from six clusters of reported income:

1. Less than $20,000 (*n* = 108)
2. Less than $40,000 (*n* = 213)
3. Less than $60,000 (*n* = 179)
4. Less than $80,000 (*n* = 144)
5. Less than $100,000 (*n* = 103)
6. $100,000 or more (*n* = 230)

Figure 9.2 shows the bar graphs of health, money, and loneliness scores for
these six income clusters, with lower incomes reporting more stressors from
all three sources.

Table 9.1. Demographics and Life Stressors

Demographic	*Health Stressors*			*Money Stressors*			*Loneliness Stressors*		
	beta	t	p <	beta	t	p <	beta	t	p <
Age	.090	2.37	.019	−.113	3.17	.003	−.201	5.61	.001
Male (1 = yes, 0 = no)	−.054	1.64	.102	−.087	2.82	.006	−.051	1.65	.101
Black (1) vs. White (0)	−.009	.27	.789	−.037	1.24	.217	−.069	2.29	.023
Asian (1) vs. White (0)	.066	2.07	.040	−.038	1.29	.199	.012	.41	.683
Other (1) vs. White (0)	.019	.57	.569	.073	2.39	.018	.043	1.41	.159
Latino (1 = yes, 0 = no)	−.018	.55	.585	.009	.31	.760	.022	.72	.472
College (1 = yes, 0 = no)	−.022	.62	.540	−.104	3.16	.003	−.010	.31	.757
Full-time (1 = yes, 0 = no)	−.105	3.02	.004	.005	.16	.877	−.078	2.38	.018
Yearly income	.137	3.51	.001	−.339	9.20	.001	−.151	4.12	.001
Partner (1 = yes, 0 = no)	−.030	.81	.420	−.013	.38	.709	−.232	6.65	.001
Household others	.061	1.62	.106	.079	2.28	.024	.062	1.77	.078
Social media (hours/day)	.071	2.08	.039	.076	2.40	.018	.025	.78	.437
Military (1 = yes, 0 = no)	−.033	1.03	.303	−.025	.82	.413	.004	.12	.902
Med. city (1) vs. Urban (0)	−.026	.67	.506	−.087	2.39	.018	.010	.28	.782
Small town (1) vs. Urban (0)	.042	1.09	.277	−.069	1.90	.058	−.003	.09	.930
Rural (1) vs. Urban (0)	.016	.43	.668	−.116	3.42	.001	.015	.43	.666
Conservatism (1–7 rating)	−.147	4.56	.001	−.011	.35	.725	−.062	2.06	.041

Adj. R^2 = .078	*Adj. R^2 = .194*	*Adj. R^2 = .184*
$F_{(17, 948)}$ = 5.77	$F_{(17, 948)}$ = 14.70	$F_{(17, 948)}$ = 13.80
p < .001	*p* < .001	*p* < .001

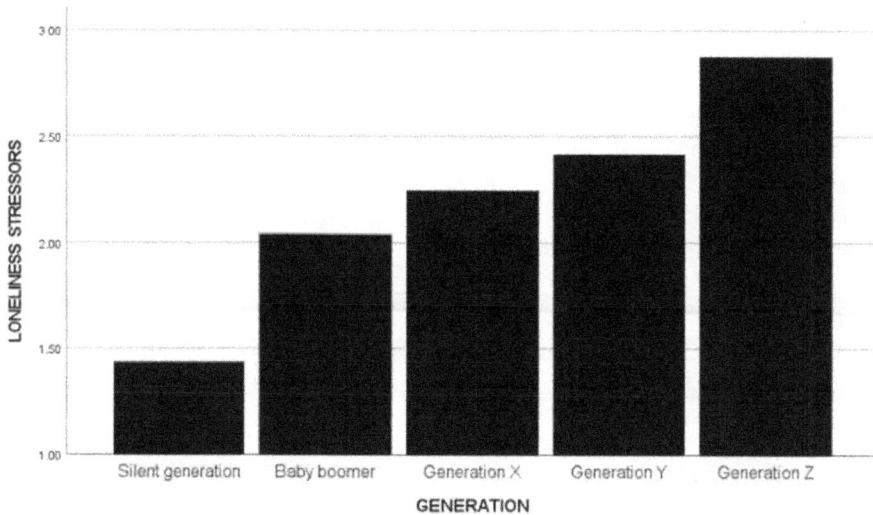

Figure 9.1. "Generations" of US citizens and loneliness stressors. *Created by the authors.*

Because partner status was found associated with loneliness stressors, we prepared a graph displaying loneliness scores for US citizens with and without a partner/spouse (n = 491, n = 486, respectively). The bar graph shown in figure 9.3 reveals higher loneliness scores for US citizens without a partner/spouse.

Because rural environment (versus urban environment) was found associated with money stressors, we prepared a graph displaying money stressor scores for US citizens from rural and urban environments (n = 95, n = 245, respectively). The bar graph shown in figure 9.4 reveals higher money stressors for US citizens in urban environments.

Finally, because conservatism ratings were found associated with health stressors, we prepared a graph displaying health stressor scores for US citizens from seven clusters according to their reported political affiliation:

1. Extremely liberal (n = 163)
2. Very liberal (n = 261)
3. Slightly liberal (n = 136)
4. Moderate (n = 189)
5. Slightly conservative (n = 87)
6. Very conservative (n = 101)
7. Extremely conservative (n = 40)

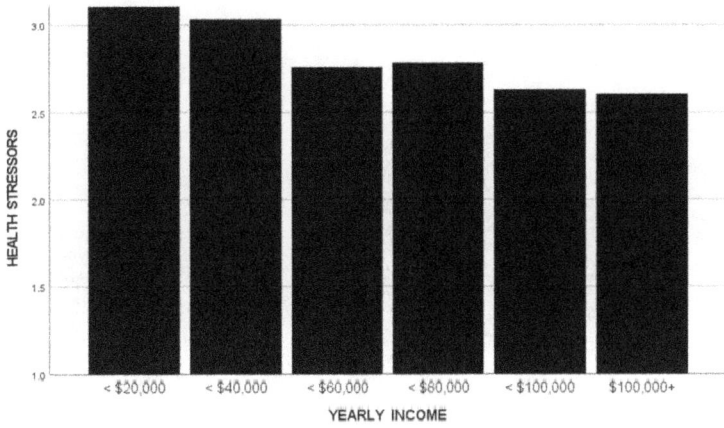

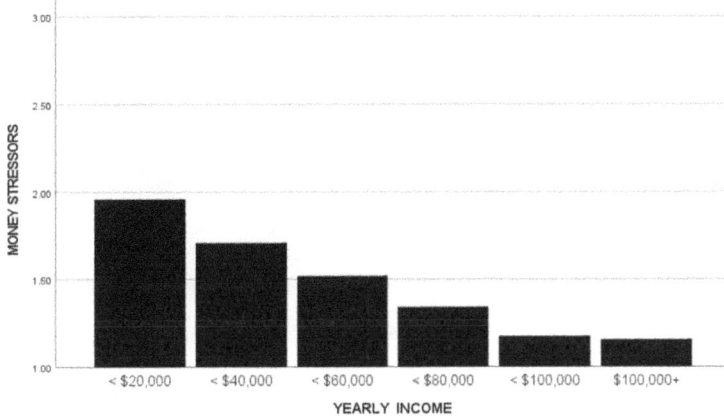

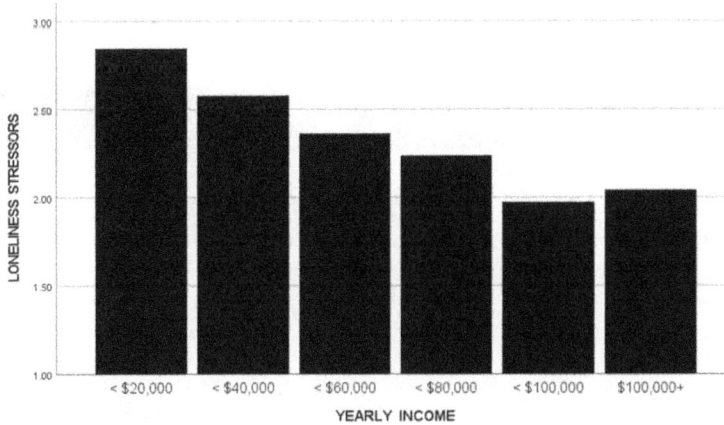

Figure 9.2. Income and health, money, loneliness stressors. *Created by the authors.*

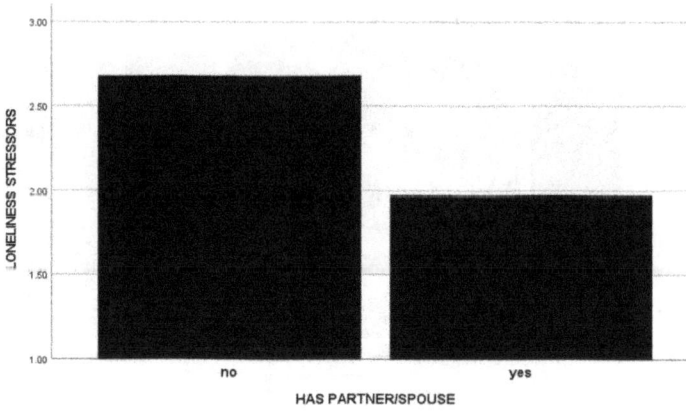

Figure 9.3. Partner status and loneliness stressors. *Created by the authors.*

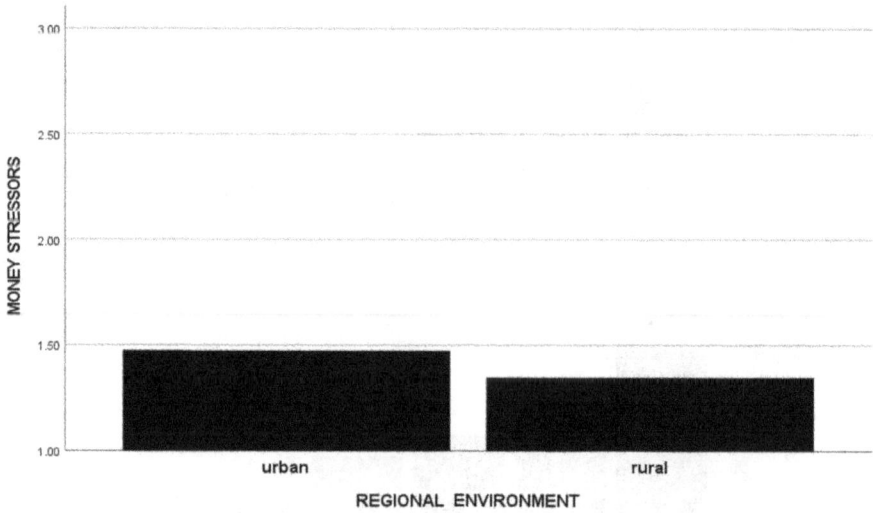

Figure 9.4. Regional environment and money stressors. *Created by the authors.*

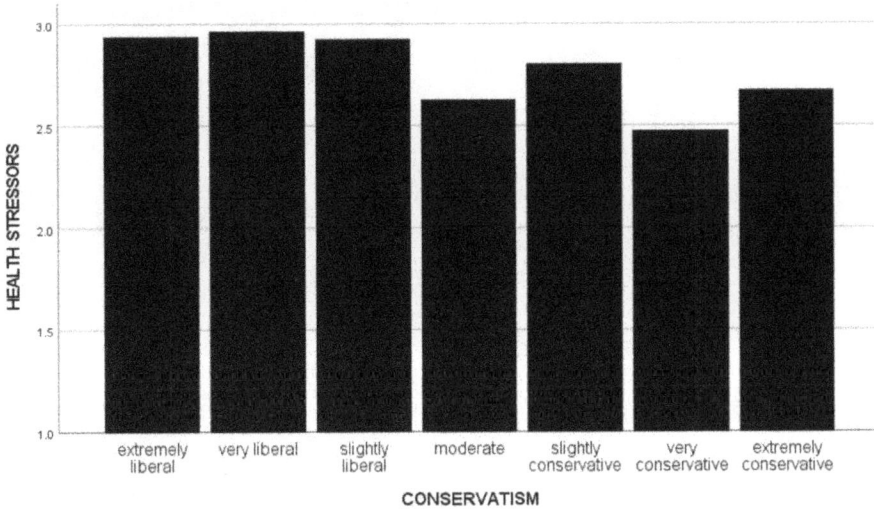

Figure 9.5. Conservatism and health stressors. *Created by the authors.*

Figure 9.5 shows the bar graph for health stressor scores for these seven clusters of political affiliation, with more liberal US citizens reporting more health stressors.

Chapter 10

Demographics and PTSD (Powerlessness)

STATISTICAL ANALYSIS

Examination of how the thirteen participant demographics were associated with PTSD as a measure of displayed powerlessness was done using SPSS 28 software to conduct a multiple regression analysis, with the score for PTSD serving as the outcome variable, and with the thirteen participant demographics serving as possible predictor variables. We again set our criterion for significance to the conservative value of $p < .001$ to reduce studywide Type I errors. Once again, these multiple regression analyses evaluate the *unique* contribution of each predictor variable once the other predictors are already taken into account. PTSD was measured as described in chapter 8 with a numerical variable that ranged from 1.00 to 5.00. The thirteen demographic variables evaluated as possible predictors of PTSD were measured as described in chapter 7. They included age, gender identity, racial identity, Latino ethnic identity, college education, full-time employment, yearly income, partner status, household size, social media exposure, military experience, regional environment, and conservative political affiliation.

Table 10.1 shows results for the multiple regression analyses to examine how participant demographics were associated with PTSD as a measure of displayed powerlessness. Using our conservative criterion for significance ($p < .001$), more PTSD symptoms were reported by those who were younger, female, with more hours per day on social media.

Chapter 10

Table 10.1. Demographics and PTSD (Powerlessness)

Demographic	PTSD		
	beta	t	p <
Age	−.262	7.19	.001
Male (1 = yes, 0 = no)	−.121	3.82	.001
Black (1) vs. White (0)	−.101	3.28	.002
Asian (1) vs. White (0)	−.038	1.24	.218
Other (1) vs. White (0)	.018	.59	.555
Latino (1 = yes, 0 = no)	−.003	.10	.918
College (1 = yes, 0 = no)	−.051	1.51	.133
Full-time (1 = yes, 0 = no)	−.098	2.95	.004
Yearly income	−.122	3.27	.002
Partner (1 = yes, 0 = no)	.026	.74	.460
Household others	.025	.69	.492
Social media (hours/day)	.108	3.33	.001
Military (1 = yes, 0 = no)	.001	.04	.967
Med. city (1) vs. Urban (0)	−.037	.99	.323
Small town (1) vs. Urban (0)	−.034	.91	.367
Rural (1) vs. Urban (0)	−.028	.82	.414
Conservatism (1–7 rating)	−.073	2.38	.019

$Adj. R^2 = .156$
$F_{(17, 948)} = 11.50$
$p < .001$

VISUAL EXAMINATION

To provide a more visual examination of how significant demographics in the above multiple regression were associated with PTSD (powerlessness) symptoms, we used SPSS 28 software to prepare bar graphs showing PTSD scores across clusters of study participants. For example, because age was found associated with PTSD, we prepared graphs displaying PTSD scores for five age-group clusters (or "generations") of US citizens:

1. Silent Generation—77–97 years of age ($n = 8$)
2. Baby Boomer—58–76 years of age ($n = 273$)
3. Generation X—42–57 years of age ($n = 242$)
4. Generation Y—26–41 years of age ($n = 301$)
5. Generation Z—18–25 years of age ($n = 142$)

Figure 10.1 shows the bar graph of PTSD scores for these five generations, with younger generations reporting more PTSD (powerlessness).

Because gender identify was found associated with PTSD (powerlessness) symptoms, we prepared a graph displaying PTSD scores for US citizens with

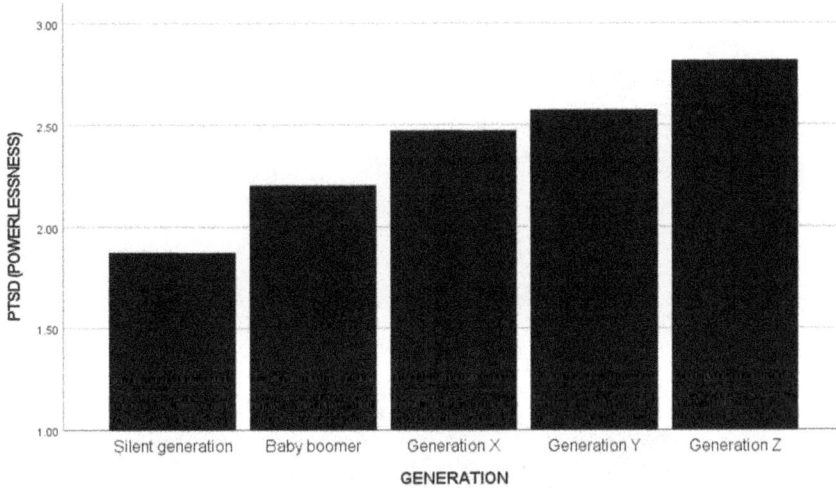

Figure 10.1. "Generations" of US citizens and PTSD (powerlessness). *Created by the authors.*

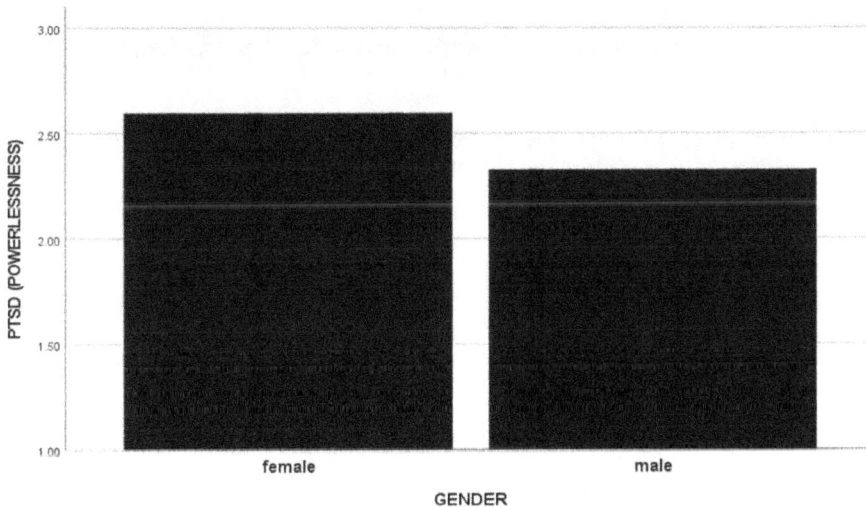

Figure 10.2. Gender and PTSD (powerlessness). *Created by the authors.*

male and female identities (*n* = 469, *n* = 498, respectively). The bar graph shown in figure 10.2 reveals more PTSD (powerless) reported by females than males.

Finally, because social media exposure was found associated with PTSD (powerlessness) symptoms, we prepared a graph displaying PTSD scores for US citizens clustered according to their reported hours/day on social media:

1. Zero hours/day ($n = 72$)
2. Up to one hour/day ($n = 325$)
3. Up to two hours/day ($n = 358$)
4. Three or more hours/day ($n = 222$)

The bar graph shown in figure 10.3 reveals more PTSD (powerless) symptoms reported by US citizens with more social media exposure.

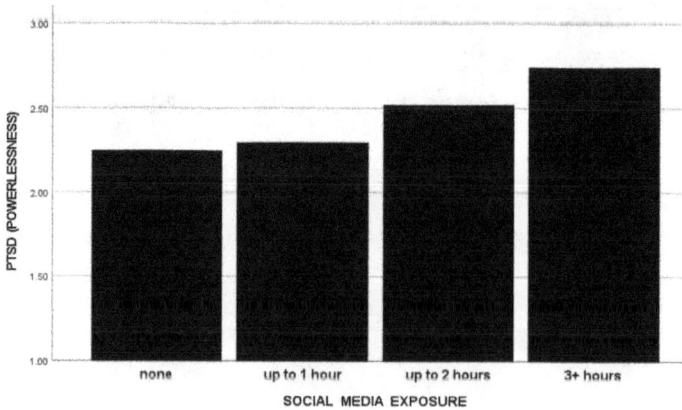

Figure 10.3. Social media exposure and PTSD (powerlessness). *Created by the authors.*

Chapter 11

Demographics and Extreme Beliefs

STATISTICAL ANALYSIS

Examination of how the thirteen participant demographics were associated with each of the five conspiracy beliefs and violent ideation was conducted with multiple regression analysis. With measures of each conspiracy belief and violent ideation serving as the outcome variable, and with the set of thirteen participant demographics serving as possible predictor variables, we again set our criterion for significance to the conservative value of $p < .001$. Violent ideation was measured as described in chapter 8 with a numerical variable that ranged from 1.00 to 5.00. The five conspiracy beliefs were also measured as described in chapter 8 with numerical variables that ranged from 1.00 to 5.00:

1. Government malfeasance
2. Malevolent world power
3. Extraterrestrial coverup
4. Personal well-being threats
5. Control of information

The thirteen participant demographics were measured as described in chapter 7. They included age, gender identity, racial identity, Latino ethnic identity, college education, full-time employment, yearly income, partner status, household size, social media exposure, military experience, regional environment, and conservative political affiliation.

Table 11.1 shows results for the multiple regressions that examined how participant demographics were associated with the six extreme beliefs. Using our conservative criterion for significance ($p < .001$), more government malfeasance beliefs were reported by participants who were younger, with no

Table 11.1. Demographics and Extreme Beliefs

Demographic	Government Malfeasance			Malevolent World Power			Extra-terrestrial Cover-up			Personal Well-Being Threat			Control of Information			Violent Ideation		
	beta	t	p <	beta	t	p <	beta	t	p <	beta	t	p <	beta	t	p <	beta	t	p <
Age	-.278	7.65	.001	-.134	3.67	.001	-.145	3.87	.001	-.135	3.79	.001	-.243	6.62	.001	-.170	4.61	.001
Male (1 = yes, 0 = no)	-.038	1.19	.236	-.059	2.15	.033	-.042	1.30	.197	-.082	2.65	.009	-.331	.96	.336	.227	7.07	.001
Black (1) vs. White (0)	.094	3.06	.003	.129	4.15	.001	.098	3.10	.003	.152	5.02	.001	.345	1.45	.148	.054	1.71	.088
Asian (1) vs. White (0)	.051	1.67	.093	.095	3.09	.003	.050	1.60	.111	.049	1.64	.102	-.301	.04	.969	.027	.88	.383
Other (1) vs. White (0)	.017	.55	.586	.015	.49	.622	.022	.68	.495	.026	.87	.388	.312	.39	.700	.033	1.04	.302
Latino (1 = yes, 0 = no)	.028	.91	.366	.042	1.33	.186	.061	1.89	.060	.059	1.90	.059	.220	.62	.536	.061	1.89	.060
College (1 = yes, 0 = no)	-.147	4.35	.001	-.132	3.93	.001	-.152	4.40	.001	-.145	4.43	.001	-.122	3.61	.001	-.088	2.58	.011
Full-time (1 = yes, 0 = no)	-.014	.41	.681	.039	1.18	.240	.053	1.55	.122	.019	.57	.570	-.017	.51	.612	.008	.25	.807
Yearly income	-.111	2.97	.004	-.115	3.06	.003	-.079	2.06	.041	-.095	2.61	.010	-.063	1.67	.096	-.035	.92	.357
Partner (1 = yes, 0 = no)	.054	1.51	.131	.048	1.34	.180	.059	1.53	.127	.048	1.38	.168	.012	.34	.735	.034	.94	.346
Household others	-.010	.28	.780	.004	.10	.921	-.039	1.05	.294	.000	.00	.998	.004	.12	.906	.009	.25	.801
Social media (hours/day)	.049	1.49	.137	.058	1.77	.078	.101	3.01	.004	.054	1.68	.094	.008	.24	.814	.130	3.92	.001
Military (1 = yes, 0 = no)	.041	1.35	.175	.018	.58	.565	.029	.92	.360	.023	.77	.443	.035	1.13	.259	.060	1.92	.056
Med. city (1) vs. Urban (0)	-.011	.29	.765	-.067	1.78	.076	-.061	1.60	.111	-.073	2.01	.046	-.014	.37	.711	.030	.83	.408
Small town (1) vs. Urban (0)	-.008	.21	.835	-.038	1.01	.312	.001	.02	.985	-.078	2.13	.034	-.008	.20	.841	.020	.59	.558
Rural (1) vs. Urban (0)	.024	.71	.482	-.032	.93	.352	.041	1.15	.251	-.007	.22	.829	.018	.53	.600	.038	.96	.339
Conservatism (1–7 rating)	.188	6.14	.001	.265	8.55	.001	.113	3.56	.001	.321	10.67	.001	.271	8.73	.001	.075	2.39	.018
	Adj. R^2 = .162 $F_{(17, 948)}$ = 11.97 $p < .001$			Adj. R^2 = .148 $F_{(17, 948)}$ = 10.83 $p < .001$			Adj. R^2 = .106 $F_{(17, 948)}$ = 7.71 $p < .001$			Adj. R^2 = .191 $F_{(17, 948)}$ = 14.32 $p < .001$			Adj. R^2 = .142 $F_{(17, 948)}$ = 10.41 $p \le .001$			Adj. R^2 = .128 $F_{(17, 948)}$ = 9.35 $p < .001$		

college degree, and with more conservative political affiliation. More malevolent world power beliefs were reported by those who were younger, with Black racial identity (as opposed to White), with no college degree, and more conservative politics. More extraterrestrial coverup beliefs were reported by those who were younger, with no college degree, and more conservative politics. More personal well-being threat beliefs were reported by those who were younger, with Black racial identity (as opposed to White), with no college degree, and with more conservative politics. More control of information beliefs were reported by those who were younger, with no college, and with more conservative politics. More violent ideation was reported by those who were younger, male, and with more social media hours.

VISUAL EXAMINATION

To provide a more visual examination of how significant demographics in the above multiple regression analyses were associated with extreme beliefs, we used SPSS 28 software to prepare bar graphs showing extreme belief scores across clusters of study participants. For example, because age was found associated with all six extreme beliefs evaluated, we prepared graphs displaying the belief scores for five age-group clusters (or "generations") of US citizens:

1. Silent Generation—77–97 years of age ($n = 8$)
2. Baby Boomer—58–76 years of age ($n = 273$)
3. Generation X—42–57 years of age ($n = 242$)
4. Generation Y—26–41 years of age ($n = 301$)
5. Generation Z—18–25 years of age ($n = 142$)

Figure 11.1 shows the bar graphs for each extreme belief across these five generations, with younger generations consistently reporting the most extreme beliefs.

Because gender was found associated with violent ideation, we prepared a graph displaying violent ideation scores for US citizens with male and female identity ($n = 469$, $n = 498$, respectively). The bar graph shown in figure 11.2 reveals more violent ideation by males.

Because having Black racial identity (as opposed to White identity) was found associated with more beliefs of malevolent world power and personal well-being threat, we prepared graphs displaying these two beliefs scores for US citizens with Black and White racial identity ($n = 120$, $n = 761$, respectively). The bar graphs shown in figure 11.3 displays these two conspiracy beliefs as being stronger by Black study participants.

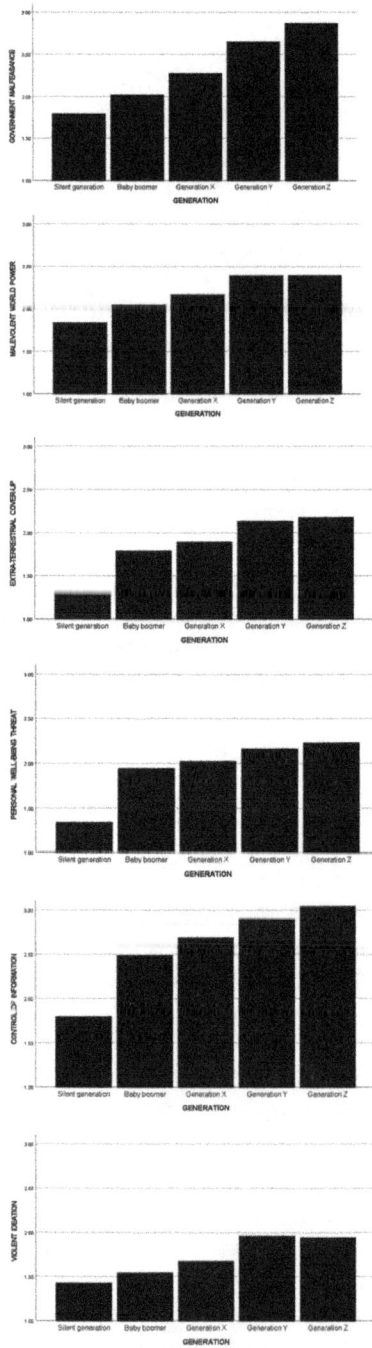

Figure 11.1. "Generations" of US citizens and extreme beliefs. *Created by the authors.*

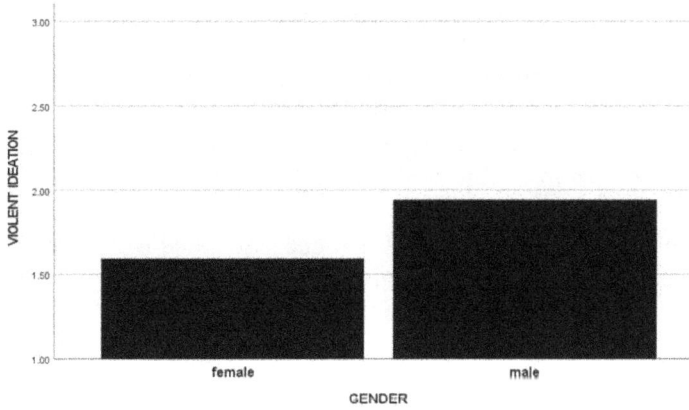

Figure 11.2. Gender and violent ideation. *Created by the authors.*

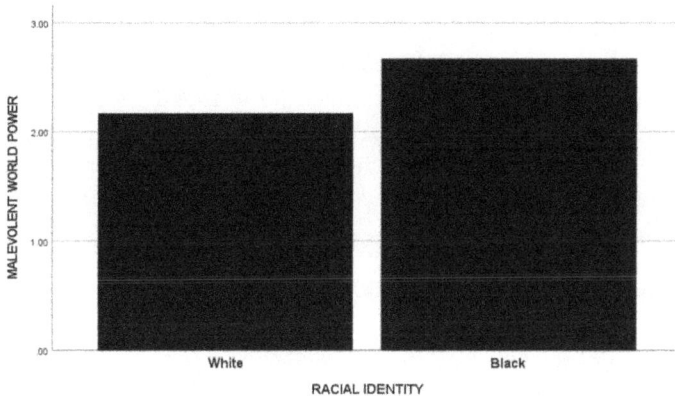

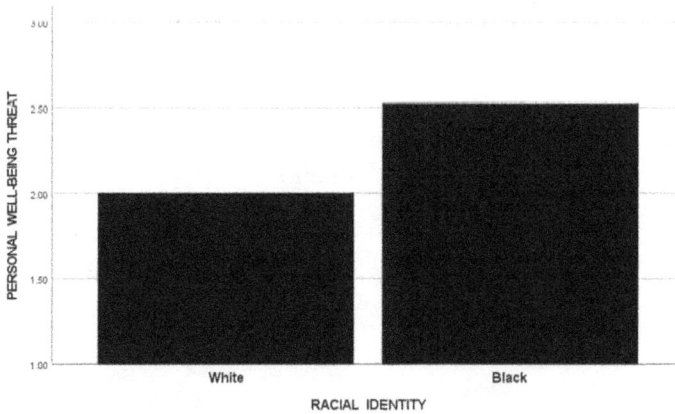

Figure 11.3. Racial identity and two conspiracy beliefs. *Created by the authors.*

Because having a college degree was found associated with all five conspiracy beliefs (government malfeasance, malevolent world power, extraterrestrial coverup, personal well-being threat, control of information), we prepared a graph displaying scores for each of these five beliefs for US citizens with and without a college degree ($n = 544$, $n = 433$, respectively). The bar graph shown in figure 11.4 reveals higher conspiracy belief scores for those without college degrees.

Because social media exposure was found associated with violent ideation, we prepared a graph displaying violent ideation scores for US citizens clustered according to their reported hours/day on social media:

1. Zero hours/day ($n = 72$)
2. Up to one hour/day ($n = 325$)
3. Up to two hours/day ($n = 358$)
4. Three or more hours/day ($n = 222$)

The bar graph shown in figure 11.5 reveals more violent ideation reported by US citizens with more social media exposure.

Finally, because conservatism ratings were found associated with the five conspiracy beliefs, we prepared a graph displaying each of these belief scores for US citizens from seven clusters according to their reported political affiliation:

1. Extremely liberal ($n = 163$)
2. Very liberal ($n = 261$)
3. Slightly liberal ($n = 136$)
4. Moderate ($n = 189$)
5. Slightly conservative ($n = 87$)
6. Very conservative ($n = 101$)
7. Extremely conservative ($n = 40$)

Figure 11.6 shows the bar graph for conspiracy belief scores for these seven clusters of political affiliation, with the most conservative US citizens reporting stronger conspiracy beliefs of all five types.

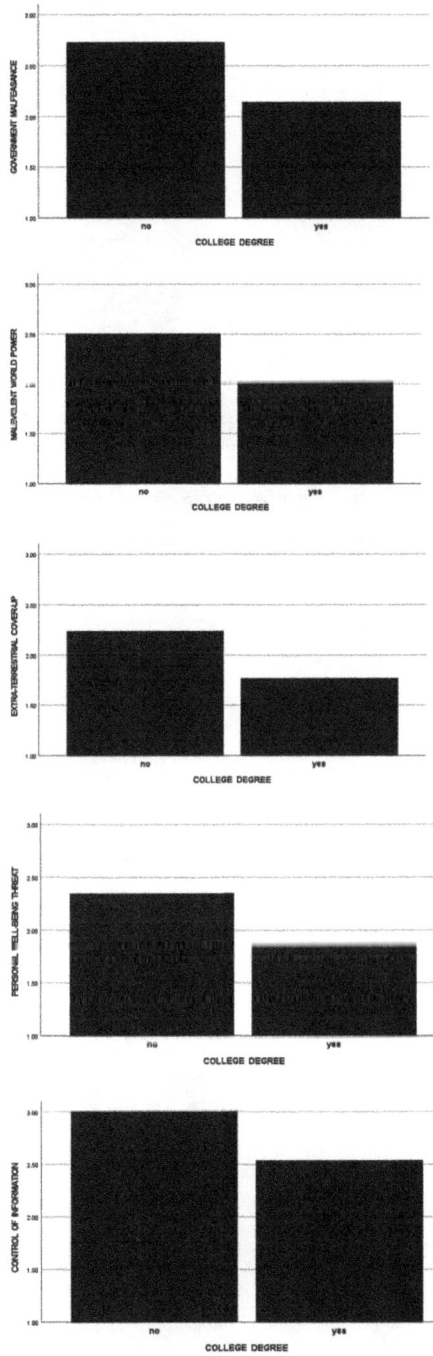

Figure 11.4. College and five conspiracy beliefs. *Created by the authors*.

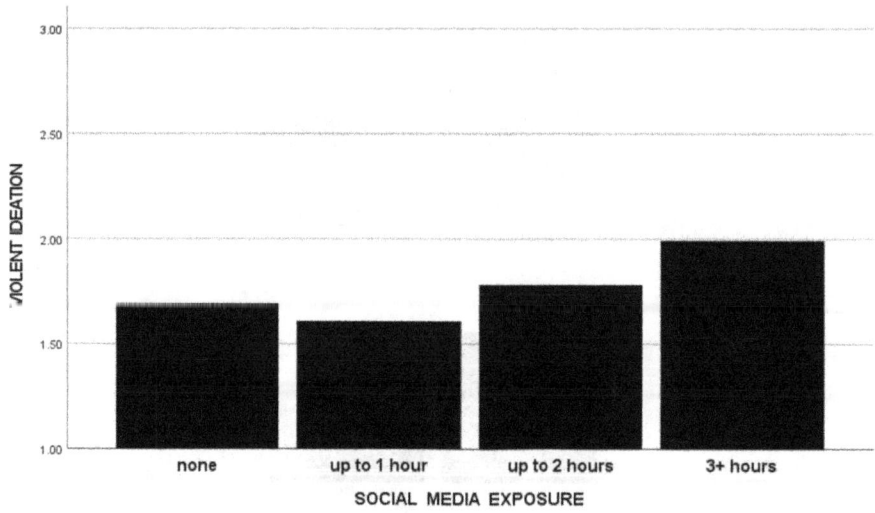

Figure 11.5. Social media exposure and violent ideation. *Created by the authors.*

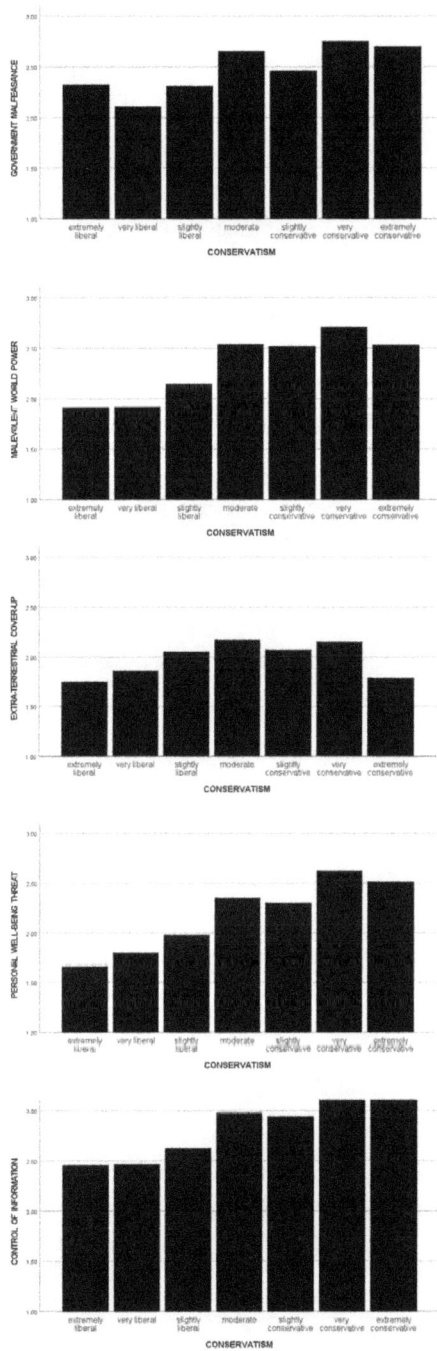

Figure 11.6. Conservatism and five conspiracy beliefs. *Created by the authors.*

Chapter 12

Life Stressors and PTSD (Powerlessness)

STATISTICAL ANALYSIS

For examination of how the three life stressors (health, money, loneliness) were associated with PTSD, our measure of *displayed* powerlessness, we conducted a multiple regression analysis with PTSD serving as the outcome variable, and with the three life stressors serving as possible predictor variables, with our criterion for significance to the conservative value of $p < .001$. Health stressors, money stressors, social stressors, and PTSD were measured as described in chapter 8 with numerical values that ranged from 1.00 to 5.00.

Table 12.1 shows results for the multiple regression analyses to examine how the three life stressors were associated with PTSD. Using our conservative criterion for significance ($p < .001$), the results indicated that all three of the life stressors (health, money, loneliness) were significantly associated with more PTSD symptoms. Loneliness stressors showed the strongest relationship to PTSD with the highest beta value (.435) in comparison to those of health stressors (.272) and money stressors (.143).

Table 12.1. Life Stressors and PTSD (Powerlessness)

Life Stressors	PTSD		
	beta	t	p <
Health stressors	.272	10.39	.001
Money stressors	.143	5.38	.001
Loneliness stressors	.435	16.15	.001
	Adj. R^2 = .436		
	$F_{(3, 973)}$ = 252.05		
	$p < .001$		

101

VISUAL EXAMINATION

To provide a more visual examination of how life stressors were associated with PTSD (powerlessness) symptoms in the above multiple regression analysis, we used SPSS 28 software to prepare a scatterplot with best-fit line for each significant association. Figure 12.1 shows the relationship between health stressors and PTSD, figure 12.2 shows the relationship between money stressors and PTSD, and figure 12.3 shows the relationship between loneliness stressors and PTSD. Visual inspection of these graphs suggests that the 977 US citizens of the present study reported more PTSD (powerlessness) symptoms when they experienced more health, money, and loneliness stressors.

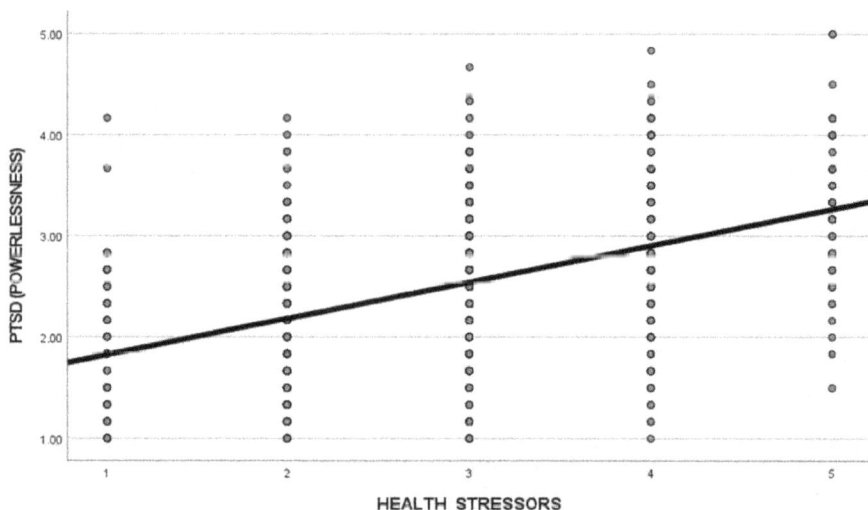

Figure 12.1. Health stressors and PTSD (powerlessness). *Created by the authors.*

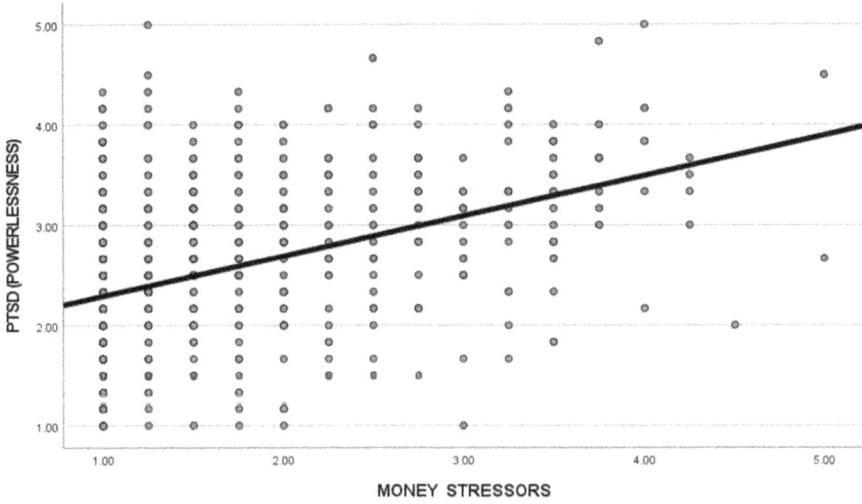

Figure 12.2. Money stressors and PTSD (powerlessness). *Created by the authors.*

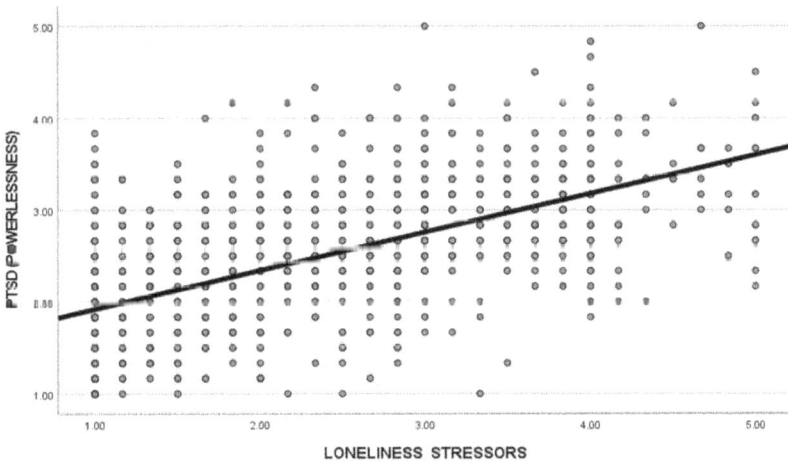

Figure 12.3. Loneliness stressors and PTSD (powerlessness). *Created by the authors.*

Chapter 13

Life Stressors and Extreme Beliefs

STATISTICAL ANALYSIS

Examination of how the three life stressors (health, money, loneliness) were associated with each of the five conspiracy beliefs and violent ideation was done using SPSS 28 software to conduct multiple regression analysis. With measures of each conspiracy belief and violent ideation serving as the outcome variable, and with the three life stressors serving as possible predictor variables, we again set our criterion for significance to the conservative value of $p < .001$ to reduce the possibility of studywise Type I errors. Once again, these multiple regression analyses evaluate the *unique* contribution of each predictor variable once the other predictors are already taken into account. Variables were measured as described in chapter 8. The three life stressors included:

1. Health stressors—a numerical variable from 1.00 to 5.00
2. Money stressors—a numerical variable from 1.00 to 5.00
3. Loneliness stressors—a numerical variable from 1.00 to 5.00

Violent ideation was measured as a numerical variable that ranged from 1.00 to 5.00. The five conspiracy beliefs included:

1. Government malfeasance—a numerical variable from 1.00 to 5.00
2. Malevolent world power—a numerical variable from 1.00 to 5.00
3. Extraterrestrial coverup—a numerical variable from 1.00 to 5.00
4. Personal well-being threat—a numerical variable from 1.00 to 5.00
5. Control of information—a numerical variable from 1.00 to 5.00

Table 13.1 shows results for the multiple regression analyses to examine how the three life stressors were associated with the five conspiracy beliefs and violent ideation. Using our conservative criterion for significance ($p <$ .001), health stressors were not significantly associated with any of the five conspiracy beliefs or violent ideation. However, more money stressors were associated with greater belief in all conspiracy theories as well as violent ideation. Additionally, more loneliness stressors were associated with greater belief in government malfeasance, personal well-being threat, and control of information, as well as more violent ideation.

VISUAL EXAMINATION

To provide a more visual examination of the life stressors significantly associated with conspiracy beliefs and violent ideation in the above multiple regression analyses, we used SPSS 28 software to prepare a scatterplot with best-fit line for each significant association. Figure 13.1 shows the relationship between money stressors and all five conspiracy beliefs (government malfeasance, malevolent world power, extraterrestrial coverup, personal well-being threat, control of information) and violent ideation. Figure 13.2 shows the relationship between loneliness stressors and three conspiracy beliefs (government malfeasance, personal well-being threat, control of information) and violent ideation. Visual inspection of these graphs suggests that the 977 US citizens of the present study adopted more extreme beliefs when they experienced more money and loneliness stressors.

Table 13.1. Life Stressors and Extreme Beliefs

Life Stressors	Government Malfeasance			Malevolent World Power		
	beta	t	p <	beta	t	p <
Health stressors	−.075	2.24	.026	−.048	1.43	.155
Money stressors	.216	6.42	.001	.203	5.92	.001
Loneliness stressors	.164	4.78	.001	.094	2.71	.008

$$Adj.\ R^2 = .085 \qquad\qquad Adj.\ R^2 = .055$$
$$F_{(3,\ 973)} = 31.18 \qquad\qquad F_{(3,\ 973)} = 19.89$$
$$p < .001 \qquad\qquad\qquad p < .001$$

Life Stressors	Extraterrestrial Coverup			Personal Well-Being Threat		
	beta	t	p <	beta	t	p <
Health stressors	−.033	.97	.336	−.061	1.81	.072
Money stressors	.192	5.61	.001	.215	6.33	.001
Loneliness stressors	.107	3.07	.003	.126	3.64	.001

$$Adj.\ R^2 = .056 \qquad\qquad Adj.\ R^2 = .070$$
$$F_{(3,\ 973)} = 10.20 \qquad\qquad F_{(3,\ 973)} = 25.53$$
$$p < .001 \qquad\qquad\qquad p < .001$$

Life Stressors	Control of Information			Violent Ideation		
	beta	t	p <	beta	t	p <
Health stressors	−.023	.68	.500	−.063	1.88	.061
Money stressors	.157	4.63	.001	.129	3.80	.001
Loneliness stressors	.186	5.40	.001	.225	6.52	.001

$$Adj.\ R^2 = .074 \qquad\qquad Adj.\ R^2 = .075$$
$$F_{(3,\ 973)} = 27.01 \qquad\qquad F_{(3,\ 973)} = 27.43$$
$$p < .001 \qquad\qquad\qquad p < .001$$

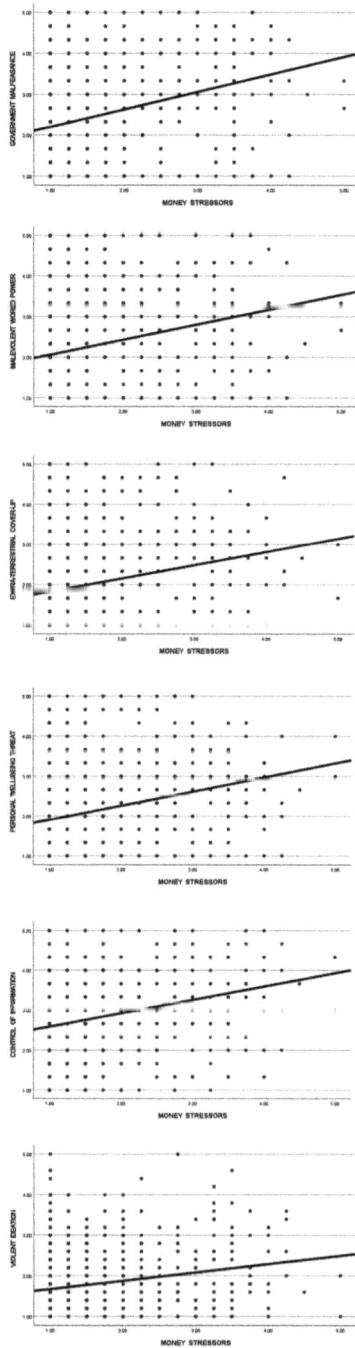

Figure 13.1. Money stressors and extreme beliefs. *Created by the authors.*

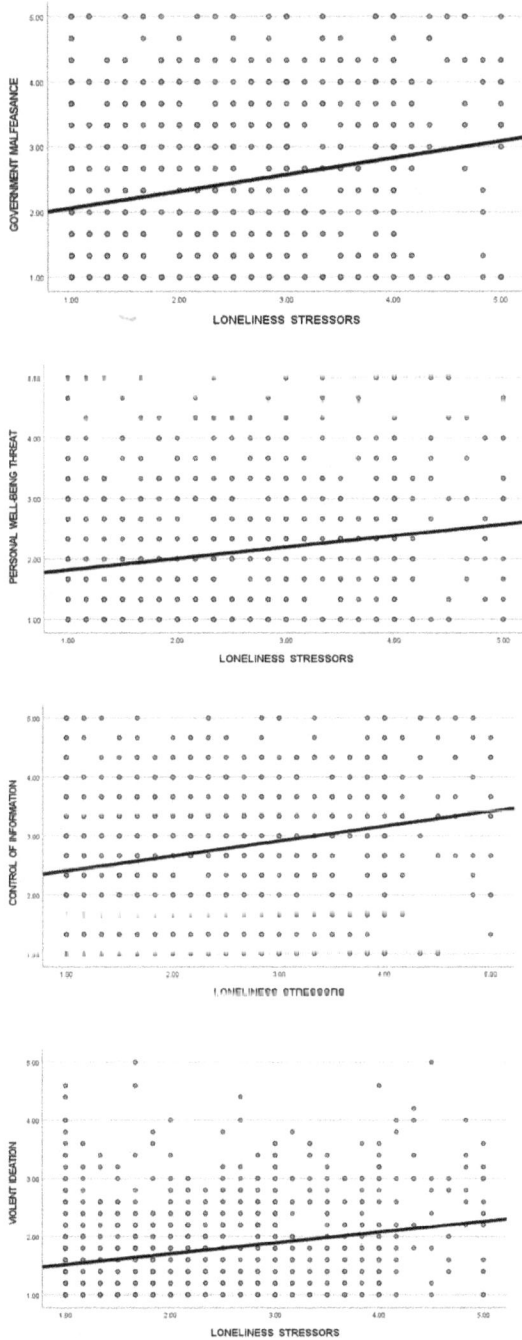

Figure 13.2. Loneliness stressors and extreme beliefs. *Created by the authors*.

Chapter 14

Five Conspiracy Beliefs
and Violent Ideation

STATISTICAL ANALYSIS

Although table 8.1 shows significant ($p < .001$) bivariate correlations between violent ideation and each of the five conspiracy beliefs (government malfeasance, malevolent world power, extraterrestrial coverup, personal well-being threat, control of information), we wanted also to examine which of the five conspiracy beliefs demonstrated a *unique* contribution to explaining the variance of violent ideation once the other conspiracy beliefs were already taken into account. Therefore, we conducted a multiple regression analysis with violent ideation serving as the outcome variable, and with the five conspiracy beliefs serving as predictor variables, again with a conservative $p < .001$ set as the criterion for significance. Violent ideation was again measured as described in chapter 8 with a numerical variable that ranged from 1.00 to 5.00. The five conspiracy beliefs were again measured as described in chapter 8 with numerical variables that ranged from 1.00 to 5.00.

Somewhat unexpectedly, results indicated that concern about extraterrestrial coverup was the only conspiracy belief found significantly associated with more violent ideation ($p < .001$). However, the more expected government malfeasance beliefs were close to being significantly associated with violent ideation ($p < .006$), but a unique contribution to explaining violent ideation was not seen for conspiracy beliefs about malevolent world power ($p < .733$), personal well-being threat ($p < .664$), or control of information ($p < .402$). However, taken together, the five types of conspiracy beliefs explained 12.6 percent (*adjusted* $R^2 = .126$) of the variance in violent ideation reported by US citizens in our sample.

Table 14.1. Conspiracy Beliefs and Violent Ideation

Conspiracy Beliefs	Violent Ideation		
	beta	t	p <
Government malfeasance	.169	2.78	.006
Malevolent world power	.021	.34	.733
Extraterrestrial coverup	.152	3.60	.001
Personal well-being threat	.027	.44	.664
Control of information	.045	.84	.402

$$Adj.\ R^2 = .126$$
$$F_{(5,\ 971)} = 29.26$$
$$p < .001$$

VISUAL EXAMINATION

To provide a more visual examination of the conspiracy belief found significantly associated with violent ideation in the above multiple regression analysis, we used SPSS 28 software to prepare a scatterplot with best-fit line. Figure 14.1 shows the relationship between the belief in extraterrestrial coverup and violent ideation. Visual inspection of this graph suggests that the more the present 977 study participants held beliefs in extraterrestrial coverup, the more they reported a willingness to display violence when threatened.

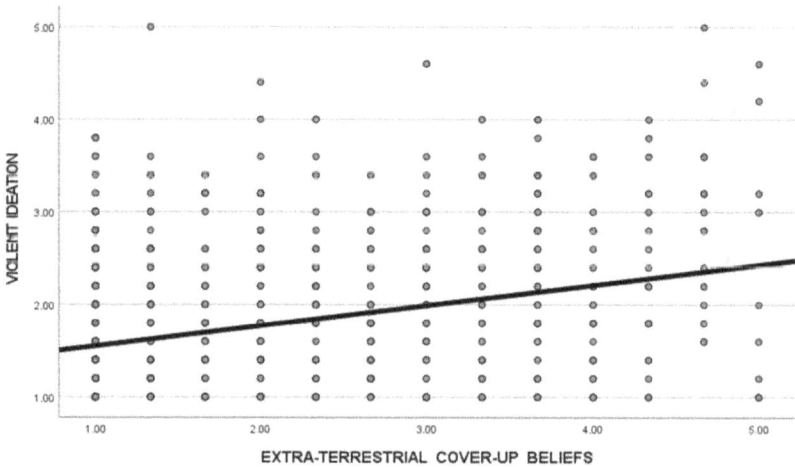

Figure 14.1. Conspiracy beliefs and violent ideation. *Created by the authors.*

Chapter 15

Does PTSD Mediate between Life Stressors and Extreme Beliefs?

THREE-VARIABLE SEQUENCE EVALUATED (*LIFE STRESSORS → PTSD → EXTREME BELIEFS*)

The threat appraisal and coping theory (Lazarus and Folkman, 1984) guided our study hypotheses that individuals who experienced intense life stressors (health, money, loneliness), combined with displayed powerlessness (PTSD), might activate cognitive coping mechanisms that make them feel more powerful, intelligent, and connected to others with similar views. We believed that the five conspiracy beliefs and violent ideation examined in the present study would serve as outcomes in this proposed process:

> *life stressor (predictor) → PTSD (mediator) → conspiracy beliefs, violent ideation (outcomes)*

We examined this three-variable sequence with bootstrapping mediational analysis using SPSS 28 software and an SPSS macro from Preacher and Hayes (2004; www.afhyes.com, www.quantpsy.org, model 4). Each of the three life stressors (health, money, loneliness) was evaluated as a predictor, PTSD was evaluated as the mediator, and each of the five conspiracy beliefs and violent ideation was evaluated as the outcome. The macro extracted 5,000 bootstrapped responses (replaced and resampled) from responses of our 977 participants to calculate 5,000 indirect effect values for each of the three-variable sequences. Each mediational analysis calculated a distribution of indirect effects found in the 5,000 bootstrapped samples, then determined whether a 99 percent confidence interval ($p < .01$) of these effects did *not* include the value of .00 (meaning *no* effect), and if so, the conclusion was reached that the three-variable sequence was significant at $p < .01$. The macro's strictest criterion for statistical significance available for the mediation effect itself is $p < .01$, but the output provides $p < .001$ values for the direct effects between pairs of variables. The macro's output also provides the mean indirect effect value calculated from the 5,000 bootstrapped samples, the standard error (*SE*) of these indirect effects, and the lower and upper values of the 99 percent confidence interval (LCI, UCI). In figures 14.1, 14.2, and 14.3, we report the direct effects between all pairs of variables (evaluated at $p < .001$), as well as three indirect values (effect size, SE, 99 percent LCI to UCI) for each three-variable sequence of *life stressor → PTSD → conspiracy belief, violent ideation*.

The three life stressors considered as predictors in these mediational analyses (health stressors, money stressors, loneliness stressors) were measured as described in chapter 8 with numerical variables that ranged from 1.00 to 5.00. PTSD considered as the mediator in these mediational analyses was measured as described in chapter 8 with a numerical variable from 1.00 to 5.00. Violent ideation and the five conspiracy beliefs (government malfeasance, malevolent world power, extraterrestrial coverup, personal well-being threat, control of information) considered as outcomes in these mediational analyses were measured as described in chapter 8 with numerical variables that ranged from 1.00 to 5.00.

PTSD AS MEDIATOR BETWEEN HEALTH STRESSORS AND EXTREME BELIEFS

Figure 15.1 shows results from bootstrapping mediational analysis that considered *health stressors* as the predictor, PTSD as the mediator, and each of the five conspiracy beliefs and violent ideation as outcomes. *All of these mediations were significant.* Also, it can be noted that in all of these analyses, the *direct* relationships between health stressors and the cognitive outcomes were not significant, whereas when health stressors were combined with PTSD, the *mediated* relationships between health stressors and the cognitive outcomes jumped into significance. These results support the idea that PTSD is the "link" between health stressors and all six extreme beliefs considered.

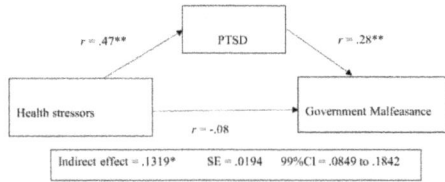

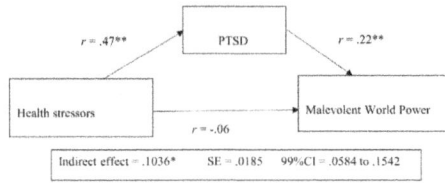

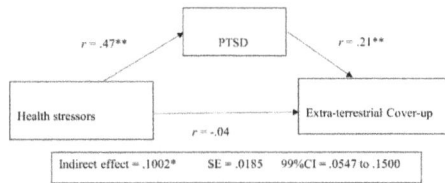

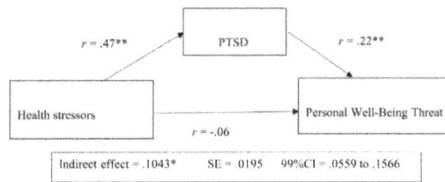

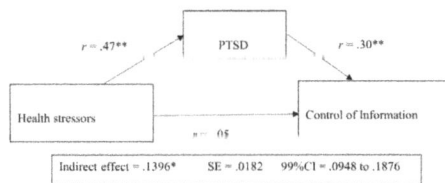

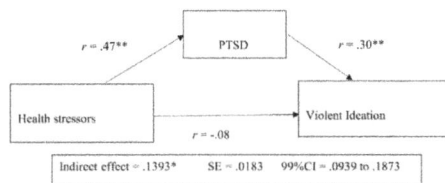

Figure 15.1. PTSD as mediator between health stressors and extreme beliefs. *Results from 5,000 bootstrapped samples using responses of 977 US citizens. Arrows show direct effects, with indirect effect shown in box below the diagram. All values are standardized coefficients. (*p < .01, **p < .001). Created by the authors.*

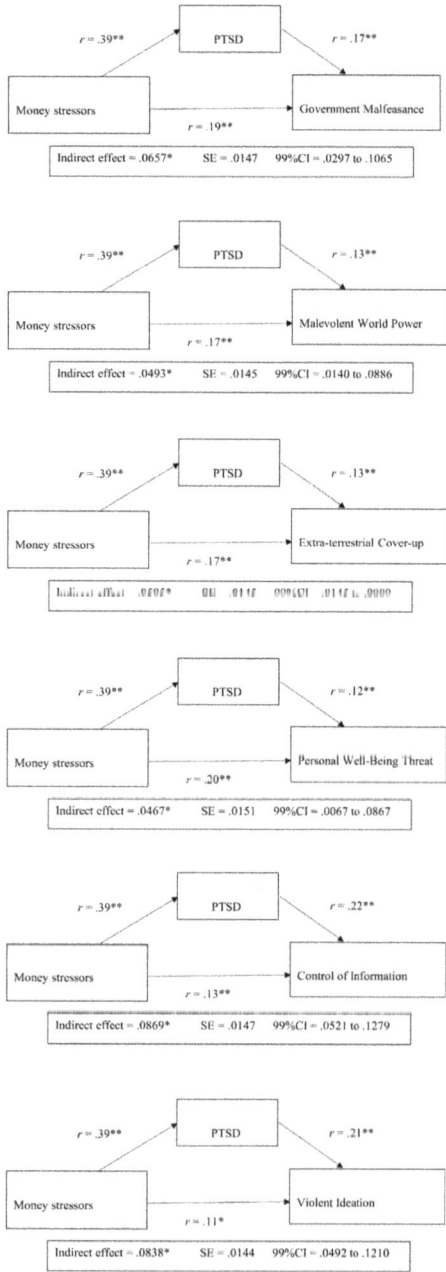

Figure 15.2. PTSD as mediator between money stressors and extreme beliefs. *Results from 5,000 bootstrapped samples using responses of 977 US citizens. Arrows show direct effects, with indirect effect shown in box below the diagram. All values are standardized coefficients. (*p < .01, **p < .001). Created by the authors.*

PTSD AS MEDIATOR BETWEEN MONEY
STRESSORS AND EXTREME BELIEFS

Figure 15.2 shows results from bootstrapping mediational analysis that considered *money stressors* as the predictor, PTSD as the mediator, and each of the five conspiracy beliefs and violent ideation as outcomes. *All of these mediations were significant.* It can also be noted that for all these analyses except those for violent ideation, the *direct* relationships between money stressors and the cognitive outcomes were significant, but then so were the PTSD *mediated* relationships between money stressors and the cognitive outcomes. These results support the idea that PTSD is a "link" between money stressors and all six extreme beliefs considered.

PTSD AS MEDIATOR BETWEEN LONELINESS
STRESSOR AND EXTREME BELIEFS

Figure 15.3 shows results from bootstrapping mediational analysis that considered *loneliness stressors* as the predictor, PTSD as the mediator, and each of the five conspiracy beliefs and violent ideation as outcomes. *All of these mediations were significant.* Also, it can be noted that in all of these analyses, the *direct* relationships between loneliness stressors and the cognitive outcomes were not significant, whereas when loneliness stressors were combined with PTSD, the *mediated* relationships between loneliness and the cognitive outcomes jumped into significance. These results support the idea that PTSD is the "link" between loneliness and all six extreme beliefs considered.

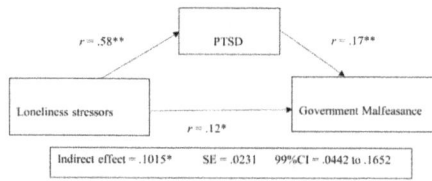

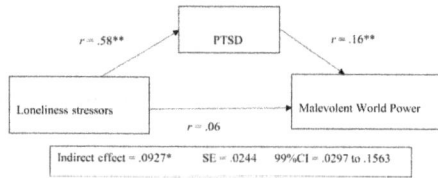

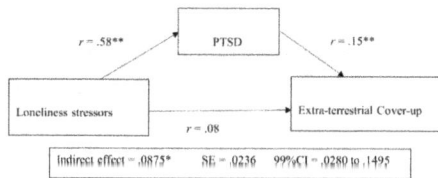

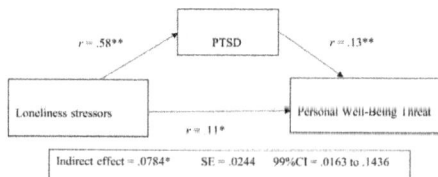

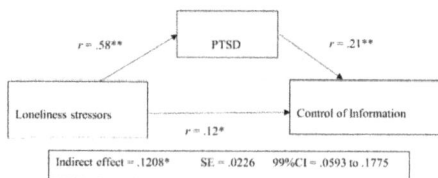

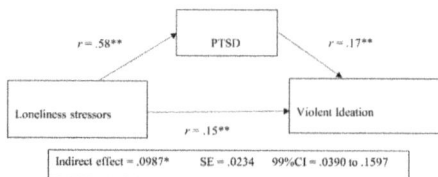

Figure 15.3. PTSD as mediator between loneliness stressors and extreme beliefs. *Results from 5,000 bootstrapped samples using responses of 977 US citizens. Arrows show direct effects, with indirect effect shown in box below the diagram. All values are standardized coefficients. (*p < .01, **p < .001). Created by the authors.*

Chapter 16

Do Demographics Moderate the Three-Variable Mediations?

DEMOGRAPHICS EVALUATED AS MODERATORS

To evaluate whether the significance of the three-variable sequences (*life stressor PTSD extreme beliefs of conspiracy, violent ideation*) varied according to participant demographics, we used SPSS 28 software and the SPSS macro provided by Preacher and Hayes to conduct moderated mediational analyses with 5,000 bootstrapped samples (2004; www.afhyes.com, www .quantpsy.org, model 7). For previous statistical analyses of the present study, we used a strict criterion of $p < .001$ for statistical significance, but this macro's strictest criterion of significance available is $p < .01$. The output from these moderated mediational analyses includes an index of moderation effect, the standard error (*SE*) of these effects, and the lower and upper values of the 99 percent confidence interval, again with this range of values not including .00 indicating that the moderation is significant ($p < .01$). We considered nine demographic variables as possible moderators, focusing our attention on those demographics found in above analyses to be significantly associated with any of our study variables (life stressors, PTSD, extreme beliefs).

These nine demographics included age, gender, racial identity (Black vs. White), college degree, yearly income, partner status, social media exposure, regional environment (rural vs. urban), and conservative political affiliation. For dichotomous variables such as gender (male = 1, female = 0), racial identity (1 = Black, 0 = White), college degree (1 = yes, 0 = no), partner status (1 = yes, 0 = no), and regional environment (1 = rural, 0 = urban), the macro compares the bootstrapped mediation effect size for participants in each of those two groups. For numbered variables such as age, income, social media hours, and conservatism rating, the macro compares the bootstrapped mediation effect size for participants at the sixteenth, fiftieth, and eighty-fourth percentiles.

DEMOGRAPHICS AS MODERATORS FOR
HEALTH STRESSORS PTSD EXTREME BELIEFS

Table 16.1 shows results for whether each of the nine demographics moderated the significant mediation found earlier for health stressors (*health stressors → PTSD → five conspiracy beliefs*, violent ideation). *None of the demographics moderated the mediations for health stressors.* These results indicate that the three-variable sequence that begins with health stressors is consistent across a wide variety of study participants.

Table 16.1. Demographics as Moderators of Health Stressors PTSD Extreme Beliefs

Extreme Belief = Government Malfeasance				
Demographic	Moderation Effect	Boot SE	99 Percent LCI to UCI	Significant (p < .01)?
Age	–.0004	.0006	–.0022 to .0012	no
Gender (male vs. female)	–.0155	.0206	–.0728 to .0378	no
Race (Black vs. White)	.0263	.0369	–.0721 to .1264	no
College degree (yes vs. no)	.0316	.0215	.0227 to .0905	no
Yearly income	–.0036	.0031	–.0120 to .0042	no
Partner status (yes vs. no)	–.0153	.0207	–.0717 to .0404	no
Social media (hours/day)	.0041	.0112	–.0250 to .0331	no
Regional environment (rural vs. urban)	.0493	.0320	.0380 to .1313	no
Conservatism rating	.0029	.0060	–.0130 to .0193	no
Extreme Belief = Malevolent World Power				
Demographic	Moderation Effect	Boot SE	99 Percent LCI to UCI	Significant (p < .01)?
Age	–.0003	.0005	–.0017 to .0009	no
Gender (male vs. female)	–.0124	.0164	–.0570 to .0290	no
Race (Black vs. White)	.0203	.0288	–.0543 to .1041	no
College degree (yes vs. no)	.0244	.0164	–.0164 to .0706	no
Yearly income	–.0028	.0025	–.0099 to .0032	no

Partner status (yes vs. no)	−.0118	.0161	−.0555 to .0304	no
Social media (hours/day)	.0032	.0087	−.0210 to .0271	no
Regional environment (rural vs. urban)	.0380	.0257	−.0316 to .1076	no
Conservatism rating	.0022	.0047	−.0104 to .0155	no

Extreme Belief = Extraterrestrial Coverup

Demographic	Moderation Effect	Boot SE	99 Percent LCI to UCI	Significant ($p < .01$)?
Age	−.0003	.0004	−.0015 to .0008	no
Gender (male vs. female)	−.0111	.0148	−.0517 to .0259	no
Race (Black vs. White)	.0177	.0253	−.0470 to .0894	no
College degree (yes vs. no)	.0212	.0148	−.0148 to .0646	no
Yearly income	−.0024	.0021	−.0083 to .0031	no
Partner status (yes vs. no)	−.0103	.0141	−.0495 to .0269	no
Social media (hours/day)	.0027	.0076	−.0177 to .0237	no
Regional environment (rural vs. urban)	.0331	.0221	−.0270 to .0964	no
Conservatism rating	.0019	.0040	−.0086 to .0132	no

Extreme Belief = Personal Well-Being Threat

Demographic	Moderation Effect	Boot SE	99 Percent LCI to UCI	Significant ($p < .01$)?
Age	−.0003	.0004	−.0015 to .0008	no
Gender (male vs. female)	−.0111	.0149	−.0532 to .0275	no
Race (Black vs. White)	.0181	.0257	−.0492 to .0930	no
College degree (yes vs. no)	.0217	.0149	.0138 to .0639	no
Yearly income	−.0025	.0022	−.0087 to .0032	no
Partner status (yes vs. no)	−.0105	.0144	−.0509 to .0273	no
Social media (hours/day)	.0028	.0077	−.0186 to .0239	no
Regional environment (rural vs. urban)	.0339	.0227	I.0292 to .0991	no
Conservatism rating	.0020	.0042	−.0093 to .0142	no

Extreme Belief = Control of Information

Demographic	Moderation Effect	Boot SE	99 Percent LCI to UCI	Significant ($p < .01$)?
Age	−.0004	.0006	−.0020 to .0011	no

Gender (male vs. female)	−.0151	.0198	−.0663 to .0379	no
Race (Black vs. White)	.0253	.0357	−.0761 to .1208	no
College degree (yes vs. no)	.0304	.0205	−.0209 to .0870	no
Yearly income	−.0035	.0029	−.0119 to .0040	no
Partner status (yes vs. no)	−.0147	.0195	−.0643 to .0366	no
Social media (hours/day)	.0039	.0107	−.0266 to .0301	no
Regional environment (rural vs. urban)	.0474	.0309	−.0327 to .1282	no
Conservatism rating	.0028	.0057	−.0116 to .0186	no

Extreme Belief = Violent Ideation

Demographic	Moderation Effect	Boot SE	99 Percent LCI to UCI	Significant (p < .01)?
Age	−.0003	.0004	−.0014 to .0008	no
Gender (male vs. female)	−.0106	.0138	−.0462 to .0251	no
Race (Black vs. White)	.0175	.0246	−.0459 to .0852	no
College degree (yes vs. no)	.0211	.0142	−.0141 to .0602	no
Yearly income	−.0024	.0020	−.0078 to .0029	no
Partner status (yes vs. no)	−.0102	.0140	−.0469 to .0275	no
Social media (hours/day)	.0027	.0073	−.0171 to .0220	no
Regional environment (rural vs. urban)	.0329	.0216	−.0232 to .0874	no
Conservatism rating	.0019	.0042	−.0092 to .0131	no

DEMOGRAPHICS AS MODERATORS FOR MONEY STRESSORS PTSD EXTREME BELIEFS

Table 16.2 shows results for whether each of the nine demographics moderated the significant mediation found earlier for money stressors (*money stressors → PTSD → five conspiracy beliefs*, violent ideation). *None of the demographics moderated the mediations for money stressors.* These results indicate that the three-variable sequence that begins with money stressors is consistent across a wide variety of study participants.

Table 16.2. Demographics as Moderators of Money Stressors PTSD Extreme Beliefs

Extreme Belief = Government Malfeasance

Demographic	Moderation Effect	Boot SE	99 Percent LCI to UCI	Significant (p < .01)?
Age	−.004	.0005	−.0019 to .0011	no
Gender (male vs. female)	.0167	.0184	−.0275 to .0717	no
Race (Black vs. White)	−.0175	.0331	−.1085 to .0723	no
College degree (yes vs. no)	.0188	.0186	−.0335 to .0715	no
Yearly income	.0040	.0035	−.0045 to .0144	no
Partner status (yes vs. no)	.0234	.0203	.0253 to .0845	no
Social media (hours/day)	.0072	.0109	−.0181 to .0409	no
Regional environment (rural vs. urban)	.0737	.0425	−.0118 to .2189	no
Conservatism rating	−.0021	.0055	−.0163 to .0138	no

Extreme Belief = Malevolent World Power

Demographic	Moderation Effect	Boot SE	99 Percent LCI to UCI	Significant (p < .01)?
Age	−.0003	.0004	−.0015 to .0008	no
Gender (male vs. female)	.0128	.0147	−.0206 to .0613	no
Race (Black vs. White)	−.0129	.0254	−.0838 to .0585	no
College degree (yes vs. no)	.0138	.0144	−.0196 to .0607	no
Yearly income	.0030	.0027	−.0030 to .0117	no
Partner status (yes vs. no)	.0172	.0161	.0191 to .0667	no
Social media (hours/day)	.0053	.0081	−.0131 to .0324	no
Regional environment (rural vs. urban)	.0543	.0337	−.0124 to .1746	no
Conservatism rating	−.0015	.0041	−.0139 to .0102	no

Extreme Belief = Extraterrestrial Coverup

Demographic	Moderation Effect	Boot SE	99 Percent LCI to UCI	Significant (p < .01)?
Age	−.0002	.0004	−.0013 to .0007	no
Gender (male vs. female)	.0123	.0133	−.0193 to .0530	no
Race (Black vs. White)	−.0119	.0235	−.0793 to .0575	no
College degree (yes vs. no)	.0128	.0130	−.0205 to .0528	no

Yearly income	.0027	.0025	−.0027 to .0112	no
Partner status (yes vs. no)	.0159	.0150	−.0176 to .0643	no
Social media (hours/day)	.0049	.0076	−.0118 to .0316	no
Regional environment (rural vs. urban)	.0501	.0303	−.0092 to .1540	no
Conservatism rating	−.0014	.0038	−.0118 to .0098	no

Extreme Belief – Personal Well-Being Threat

Demographic	Moderation Effect	Boot SE	99 Percent LCI to UCI	Significant ($p < .01$)?
Age	−.0002	.0003	−.0012 to .0006	no
Gender (male vs. female)	.0107	.0125	−.0190 to .0511	no
Race (Black vs. White)	−.0108	.0213	−.0743 to .0536	no
College degree (yes vs. no)	.0116	.0121	−.0184 to .0489	no
Yearly income	.0025	.0024	−.0029 to .0102	no
Partner status (yes vs. no)	.0144	.0136	−.0185 to .0585	no
Social media (hours/day)	.0045	.0069	−.0119 to .0272	no
Regional environment (rural vs. urban)	.0456	.0297	−.0092 to .1449	no
Conservatism rating	−.0013	.0035	−.0108 to .0090	no

Extreme Belief = Control of Information

Demographic	Moderation Effect	Boot SE	99 Percent LCI to UCI	Significant ($p < .01$)?
Age	−.0004	.0006	−.0021 to .0013	no
Gender (male vs. female)	.0203	.0216	−.0303 to .0801	no
Race (Black vs. White)	−.0210	.0403	−.1277 to .0952	no
College degree (yes vs. no)	.0226	.0217	−.0339 to .0818	no
Yearly income	.0048	.0040	−.0048 to .0163	no
Partner status (yes vs. no)	.0281	.0244	−.0310 to .0993	no
Social media (hours/day)	.0087	.0127	−.0212 to .0460	no
Regional environment (rural vs. urban)	.0886	.0495	−.0201 to .2467	no
Conservatism rating	−.0025	.0066	−.0192 to .0158	no

Extreme Belief = Violent Ideation

Demographic	Moderation Effect	Boot SE	99 Percent LCI to UCI	Significant ($p < .01$)?
Age	−.0003	.0004	−.0015 to .0008	no

Gender (male vs. female)	.0136	.0145	–.0219 to .0558	no
Race (Black vs. White)	–.0141	.0273	–.0904 to .0574	no
College degree (yes vs. no)	.0151	.0146	–.0225 to .0562	no
Yearly income	.0032	.0028	–.0034 to .0120	no
Partner status (yes vs. no)	.0188	.0162	–.0230 to .0643	no
Social media (hours/day)	.0058	.0086	–.0143 to .0323	no
Regional environment (rural vs. urban)	.0593	.0316	–.0125 to .1583	no
Conservatism rating	–.0017	.0044	–.0131 to .0105	no

DEMOGRAPHICS AS MODERATORS OF LONELINESS STRESSORS PTSD EXTREME BELIEFS

Table 16.3 shows results for whether each of the nine demographics moderates the significant mediation found earlier for loneliness stressors (*loneliness → PTSD → five conspiracy beliefs*, violent ideation). *None of the demographics moderated the mediations for loneliness stressors.* These results indicate that the three-variable sequence that begins with loneliness is consistent across a wide variety of study participants.

Table 16.3. Demographics as Moderators of Loneliness Stressors PTSD Extreme Beliefs

Extreme Belief = Government Malfeasance

Demographic	Moderation Effect	Boot SE	99 Percent LCI to UCI	Significant ($p < .01$)?
Age	.0000	.0004	–.0011 to .0009	no
Gender (male vs. female)	–.0132	.0115	–.0467 to .0155	no
Race (Black vs. White)	.0186	.0186	–.0269 to .0734	no
College degree (yes vs. no)	–.0066	.0113	–.0399 to .0230	no
Yearly income	–.0011	.0018	–.0059 to .0037	no
Partner status (yes vs. no)	.0106	.0118	–.0208 to .0447	no
Social media (hours/day)	.0017	.0059	–.0147 to .0182	no
Regional environment (rural vs. urban)	.0138	.0178	–.0368 to .0654	no
Conservatism rating	–.0067	.0038	–.0184 to .0020	no

Extreme Belief = Malevolent World Power

Demographic	Moderation Effect	Boot SE	99 Percent LCI to UCI	Significant ($p < .01$)?
Age	.0000	.0003	−.0009 to .0008	no
Gender (male vs. female)	−.0122	.0111	−.0464 to .0136	no
Race (Black vs. White)	.0167	.0173	−.0272 to .0680	no
College degree (yes vs. no)	−.0060	.0102	−.0338 to .0217	no
Yearly income	−.0010	.0016	−.0056 to .0032	no
Partner status (yes vs. no)	.0095	.0108	−.0177 to .0421	no
Social media (hours/day)	.0015	.0054	−.0128 to .0170	no
Regional environment (rural vs. urban)	.0124	.0159	−.0319 to .0592	no
Conservatism rating	−.0060	.0035	−.0171 to .0014	no

Extreme Belief = Extraterrestrial Coverup

Demographic	Moderation Effect	Boot SE	99 Percent LCI to UCI	Significant ($p < .01$)?
Age	.0000	.0003	−.0009 to .0007	no
Gender (male vs. female)	−.0105	.0095	−.0390 to .0108	no
Race (Black vs. White)	.0142	.0151	−.0244 to .0637	no
College degree (yes vs. no)	−.0051	.0085	−.0285 to .0201	no
Yearly income	−.0008	.0014	−.0048 to .0032	no
Partner status (yes vs. no)	.0081	.0095	−.0147 to .0365	no
Social media (hours/day)	.0013	.0045	−.0099 to .0144	no
Regional environment (rural vs. urban)	.0105	.0137	−.0276 to .0509	no
Conservatism rating	−.0051	.0030	−.0139 to .0014	no

Extreme Belief = Personal Well-Being Threat

Demographic	Moderation Effect	Boot SE	99 Percent LCI to UCI	Significant ($p < .01$)?
Age	.0000	.0002	−.0007 to .0007	no
Gender (male vs. female)	−.0091	.0084	−.0368 to .0098	no
Race (Black vs. White)	.0125	.0133	−.0210 to .0568	no
College degree (yes vs. no)	−.0045	.0078	−.0272 to .0185	no
Yearly income	−.0007	.0012	−.0043 to .0026	no

Partner status (yes vs. no)	.0071	.0083	−.0143 to .0318	no
Social media (hours/day)	.0011	.0040	−.0099 to .0122	no
Regional environment (rural vs. urban)	.0093	.0123	−.0244 to .0454	no
Conservatism rating	−.0045	.0028	−.0137 to .0013	no

Extreme Belief = Control of Information

Demographic	Moderation Effect	Boot SE	99 Percent LCI to UCI	Significant (*p* < .01)?
Age	.0000	.0004	−.0011 to .0010	no
Gender (male vs. female)	−.0141	.0123	−.0509 to .0169	no
Race (Black vs. White)	.0202	.0202	−.0309 to .0765	no
College degree (yes vs. no)	−.0072	.0119	−.0393 to .0238	no
Yearly income	−.0012	.0019	−.0064 to .0037	no
Partner status (yes vs. no)	.0115	.0128	−.0224 to .0474	no
Social media (hours/day)	.0018	.0063	−.0151 to .0193	no
Regional environment (rural vs. urban)	.0150	.0185	−.0352 to .0645	no
Conservatism rating	−.0073	.0039	−.0188 to .0015	no

Extreme Belief = Violent Ideation

Demographic	Moderation Effect	Boot SE	99 Percent LCI to UCI	Significant (*p* < .01)?
Age	.0000	.0002	−.0006 to .0006	no
Gender (male vs. female)	−.0085	.0075	−.0306 to .0107	no
Race (Black vs. White)	.0114	.0118	−.0160 to .0489	no
College degree (yes vs. no)	−.0041	.0070	−.0263 to .0151	no
Yearly income	−.0007	.0011	−.0037 to .0023	no
Partner status (yes vs. no)	.0065	.0075	−.0121 to .0289	no
Social media (hours/day)	.0010	.0037	−.0092 to .0114	no
Regional environment (rural vs. urban)	.0085	.0110	−.0200 to .0397	no
Conservatism rating	−.0041	.0023	−.0118 to .0010	no

PART 5

Summary and Conclusions

Chapter 17

Summary of Study Results

OVERALL SUMMARY OF FINDINGS

With the FBI announcement that the greatest threat to national security is home-grown terrorists with extreme beliefs (Solman et al., 2021), the purpose of the present study of 977 US citizens was to provide new information for the demographics of *WHO?* tends to adopt extreme beliefs, and for psychologically *WHY?* they do so. The five conspiracy theories we evaluated as extreme beliefs included government malfeasance, malevolent world power, extraterrestrial coverup, personal well-being threat, and control of information. We also evaluated as an extreme belief the individual's violent ideation or the reported willingness to commit violence when threatened.

As for *WHO?* tends to adopt extreme beliefs, results of our study of 977 US citizens in March of 2022 identified three demographic characteristics significantly associated with all five conspiracy beliefs: younger age, no college degree, and conservative political affiliation. Additionally, Black racial identity was associated with more belief in malevolent world power and personal well-being threat. Finally, three demographic characteristics were significantly associated with violent ideation: younger age, male gender, and more social media exposure.

As for *WHY?* our study participants may have been at risk for extreme beliefs, first we found they reported health and loneliness stressors as their strongest concerns. Perhaps these findings are due to the COVID-19 pandemic that study participants had endured, which had threatened their physical and social life for the previous two years. Also, we found that of the five conspiracy theories considered, study participants reported strongest belief in government malfeasance and control of information, again perhaps because of frustration with changing information and policies concerning COVID-19 they had recently experienced.

131

Additionally, to answer to the question of *WHY?* our sample of 977 US citizens might adopt conspiracy beliefs and violent ideation, our investigation evaluated a three-step process suggested by principles of the threat appraisal and coping theory (Lazarus & Folkman, 1984). The theory led us to believe that when US citizens experience intense life stressors (such as health, money, loneliness problems), especially when combined with the powerlessness symptoms of PTSD (memory problems, disordered sleep, hypervigilance, social withdrawal), those individuals might adopt extreme beliefs as "cognitive coping" mechanisms that offer them a sense of greater understanding, power, and community with like-minded others. This three-step process (*life stressors → PTSD symptoms → extreme beliefs*) was strongly supported in our sample of 977 US citizens, with the pattern found significant for all three types of stressors considered (health, money, loneliness), and for all six extreme beliefs considered (government malfeasance, malevolent world power, extraterrestrial coverup, personal well-being threat, control of information, and violent ideation). Furthermore, when important demographic characteristics were evaluated as possible moderators that might alter the three-variable cognitive sequence (age, gender, race, college, income, social media, conservatism), *none of these demographics was significant as a moderator*, suggesting an almost universality in the significance of our proposed three-step process leading to extreme beliefs.

Identification of PTSD as a persistent "link" between life stressors and extreme beliefs (*life stressors → PTSD symptoms → extreme beliefs*) may be useful for intervention efforts sought by concerned families, therapists, and governments hoping to reduce the risk for dangerous extreme beliefs, especially for US citizens most vulnerable to them (young, male, no college, extensive social media exposure, conservative politics). Fortunately, a number of treatment programs are now available to reduce PTSD symptoms (see below). Additionally, other creative interventions could be developed to reduce the health, money, and loneliness stressors that appear to start the three-variable sequence to dangerous extreme beliefs.

SUMMARY OF FINDINGS FOR
SIGNIFICANT DEMOGRAPHICS

Age

Results from the present study of 977 US citizens suggest that younger age was associated with significantly more loneliness stressors. Younger age was also associated with more reported PTSD symptoms of powerlessness with its problems with nightmares, irritability, excessive alertness, and social withdrawal. Perhaps the social lockdowns of COVID-19 made it more difficult for young adults to meet intimate partners and enjoy socializing with friends, and it may take more years of being a mature adult to develop one's own healthy coping mechanisms to deal with life stressors and PTSD symptoms. Additionally, younger adults were more likely to report *all* six extreme beliefs evaluated in the present study including five conspiracy beliefs (government malfeasance, malevolent world power, extraterrestrial coverup, personal well-being threat, control of information) and violent ideation. Our study hypothesis was that when exposure to life stressors is combined with PTSD symptoms of powerlessness, individuals may adopt extreme beliefs as coping mechanisms to enhance their sense of insight, strength, and community *(life stressors → PTSD powerlessness → extreme beliefs)*. Perhaps younger adults with fewer years behind them to have developed healthier coping behaviors (social support, exercise, altruism, spirituality, exposure to nature) could be expected to be more likely to adopt the angry certainty available in adopting extreme beliefs.

Gender

The present study found that women reported more PTSD symptoms than men, and that men reported more violent ideation than women. These patterns are similar to those of past research suggesting that females are more likely to experience PTSD symptoms (Murdoch, Spoont, Sayer, Kehle-Forbes, & Noorbaloochi, 2021), and that males are more likely to be willing to respond to life stresses with violence (dos Santos, Soares, Lima, dos Santos, Silva, Bezerra, & Garros, 2021).

Racial Identity

Results from the present sample of US citizens found that individuals with a Black racial identity reported stronger beliefs in malevolent world power and personal well-being threat than did individuals with a White racial identity. These suspicions held by Black citizens may be based on a long history of racial discrimination in housing, health care, education, employment, and law enforcement (Mus, Bor, & Bang Petersen, 2022), and they suggest that not all "conspiracy" beliefs are unfounded.

College Degree

US citizens in the present sample who had completed at least a four-year college degree were significantly less likely to hold any of the five conspiracy beliefs (government malfeasance, malevolent world power, extraterrestrial coverup, personal well-being threat, control of information). One interpretation of these patterns would be that additional formal education provided them with information, resources, and greater access to alternative coping skills for dealing with life stressors (e.g., employment opportunities, improved health care) so they were less likely to adopt extreme beliefs.

Partner Status

Results from the present study found that US citizens with a spouse or romantic partner reported significantly less loneliness stressors than did those without this type of relationship in their lives. Similarly, past research suggests that reduction of loneliness is one of the primary benefits of having an intimate partner (Moseley, Turner-Cobb, Spahr, Shields, & Slavich, 2021).

Social Media Exposure

Present study participants with more hours per day of social media exposure (Facebook, Twitter, Snapchat, etc.) reported significantly more PTSD symptoms of sleep disruption, irritability, hypervigilance, social avoidance. One interpretation of this finding would be that exposure to the idealized depictions of other people's lives displayed on social media prompts feelings of inadequacy and powerlessness to obtain such an ideal existence (Keating, Can, & Hendy, 2016). Alternatively, it could be that when individuals experience troubling PTSD symptoms, they turn to family and friends on social media for support and information for how to reduce these symptoms (Keating et al., 2016).

Another finding of the present study was that individuals with more social media exposure also reported more violent ideation, or willingness to commit violence if they believed they were threatened or their rights were violated. One interpretation of this pattern would be that when individuals use social media to share the anger they feel from social stressors they are experiencing, others on social media may offer commentary that escalates the person's irritation to rage and even to thoughts of violence.

Regional Environment

Present results from a sample of US citizens found that individuals living in urban environments reported more money stressors than did individuals living in rural environments. This pattern may be due to the higher cost of living in an urban environment such as in housing, transportation, education, food, and so on.

Conservative Political Affiliation

Results from the present study revealed that US citizens who had more conservative political affiliation reported fewer health stressors than did those with more liberal political viewpoints. One interpretation of this finding would be that conservative-leaning individuals may have relied more on news outlets that often downplayed the risks of the COVID-19 pandemic and expressed scorn for protective policies such as masks, social distancing, and vaccinations (Radnovich, 2021). In contrast, more liberal-leaning individuals may have relied more on news outlets that provided daily coverage of hospitalizations, deaths, and advice from medical experts who recommended the protective actions, prompting liberal individuals to experience and report more health stressors at the time of our survey.

SUMMARY OF FINDINGS FOR LIFE STRESSORS

Health Stressors

Demographic characteristics associated with more health stressors were low income and liberal political affiliation. Health stressors were associated with more PTSD symptoms, the mediator in our proposed three-variable sequence (*life stressors → PTSD → extreme beliefs*). Health stressors were not *directly* associated with any of the five conspiracy beliefs or violent ideation, but when combined with PTSD symptoms as the mediator, then health stressors were *indirectly* associated with each of the six extreme beliefs. Finally, none of the nine demographics considered (age, gender, race, college, income, partner status, social media exposure, regional environment, conservatism) moderated/altered these three-variable sequences that began with health stressors, suggesting they are relevant for a variety of US citizens

Money Stressors

Demographic characteristics associated with more money stressors were low income and living in an urban environment. Money stressors were significantly associated with PTSD symptoms, the mediator in our proposed three-variable sequence (*life stressors → PTSD → extreme beliefs*). Money stressors were both *directly* associated with each of the five conspiracy beliefs and violent ideation, as well as *indirectly* associated with them when combined with PTSD symptoms. Finally, none of the nine demographics considered (age, gender, race, college, income, partner status, social media exposure, regional environment, conservatism) moderated/altered these three-variable sequences that began with money stressors, which suggests their relevance for many US citizens.

Loneliness Stressors

Demographic characteristics associated with more loneliness stressors were young age, low income, and having no partner/spouse. Loneliness was significantly associated with PTSD symptoms, the mediator in our proposed three-variable sequence (*life stressors → PTSD → extreme beliefs*). Loneliness stressors were both *directly* associated with each of the five conspiracy beliefs and violent ideation as well *indirectly* associated with them when combined with PTSD symptoms. Finally, none of the nine demographics considered (age, gender, race, college, income, partner status, social media exposure, regional environment, conservatism) moderated/altered these three-variable sequences that began with loneliness stressors, which suggests their relevance for many US citizens.

SUMMARY OF FINDINGS FOR
PTSD (POWERLESSNESS)

PTSD Symptoms

Demographic characteristics associated with more PTSD symptom included younger age, female gender, and more daily hours on social media. Each of three life stressors (health, money, loneliness) explained a unique portion of the variance in PTSD symptoms even with the other stressors taken into account. PTSD was identified as a significant mediator (or "link") between each of the three life stressors and each of the six extreme behaviors considered (government malfeasance, malevolent world power, extraterrestrial cover-up, personal well-being threats, control of information, violent ideation).

SUMMARY OF FINDINGS FOR EXTREME BELIEFS

Government Malfeasance

Demographic characteristics associated with the conspiracy belief of government malfeasance were younger age, no college degree, and conservative political affiliation. Money problems and loneliness were the life stressors directly associated with government malfeasance beliefs. However, when combined with PTSD symptoms, all three life stressors (health, money, loneliness) were linked with more of these beliefs. Finally, none of the nine demographics considered (age, gender, race, college, income, partner status, social media exposure, regional environment, conservatism) moderated/ altered these three-variable sequences (*life stressors → PTSD → government conspiracy beliefs*), which supports their widespread relevance for the present sample of US citizens.

Malevolent World Power

Demographic characteristics associated with malevolent world power beliefs were younger age, Black racial identity, no college, and conservatism. Money problems were the only life stressor directly associated with malevolent world power beliefs. However, when combined with PTSD symptoms, all three life stressors (health, money, loneliness) were linked with more of these beliefs. Finally, none of the nine demographics considered (age, gender, race, college, income, partner status, social media exposure, regional environment, conservatism) moderated these three-variable sequences (*life stressors → PTSD → malevolent world power beliefs*), supporting their widespread relevance for the present sample of US citizens.

Extraterrestrial Coverup

Demographic characteristics associated with extraterrestrial coverup beliefs were younger age, no college, and conservatism. Money problems were the only life stressor directly associated with extraterrestrial coverup beliefs. However, when combined with PTSD symptoms, all three life stressors (health, money, loneliness) were linked with more of these beliefs. Finally, none of the nine demographics considered (age, gender, race, college, income, partner status, social media exposure, regional environment, conservatism) moderated these three-variable sequences (*life stressors → PTSD → extraterrestrial cover-up beliefs*), supporting their widespread relevance for the present study's sample of US citizens.

Personal Well-Being Threat

Demographic characteristics associated with conspiracy beliefs about personal well-being threats were younger age, Black racial identity, no college, and conservatism. Both money problems and loneliness were life stressors directly associated with beliefs in well-being threats. However, when combined with PTSD symptoms, all three life stressors (health, money, loneliness) were linked with more of these beliefs. Finally, none of the nine demographics considered (age, gender, race, college, income, partner status, social media exposure, regional environment, conservatism) moderated/ altered these three-variable sequences (*life stressors → PTSD → personal well-being threat beliefs*), supporting their widespread relevance for the present sample of US citizens.

Control of Information

Demographic characteristics associated with conspiracy beliefs about control of information were younger age, Black racial identity, no college, and conservatism. Both money problems and loneliness were life stressors directly associated with beliefs about control of information. However, when combined with PTSD symptoms, all three life stressors (health, money, loneliness) were linked with more of these beliefs. Finally, none of the seven demographics considered (age, gender, race, college, income, partner status, social media exposure, regional environment, conservatism) moderated/ altered these three-variable sequences (*life stressors → PTSD → control of information beliefs*), supporting their widespread relevance for the present sample of US citizens.

Violent Ideation

Demographic characteristics associated with willingness to commit violence were younger age, male gender, and social media exposure. Both money problems and loneliness were life stressors directly associated with such violent ideation. However, when combined with PTSD symptoms, all three life stressors (health, money, loneliness) were linked with more violent ideation. None of the nine demographics considered (age, gender, race, college, income, partner status, social media exposure, regional environment, conservatism) moderated these three-variable sequences (*life stressors → PTSD → violent ideation*), supporting their widespread relevance for the present sample of US citizens. Finally, bivariate correlations revealed that increased violent ideation was associated with all five conspiracy beliefs considered in the present study (government malfeasance, malevolent world power, extraterrestrial coverup, personal well-being threat, control of information), although when all these beliefs were compared for their association with violent ideation, only the belief concerning extraterrestrial coverup was significant.

Chapter 18

Interpretation and Application of Study Results

INTERPRETATION OF STUDY RESULTS

In answer to the question of *WHO?* tends to adopt conspiracy beliefs, past research suggests that those with younger age, female gender, minority racial identity, less education, and conservative politics at greater risk for extreme beliefs (Andrade, 2021; Carey 2019; Dyrendal, Kennair, & Bendixen, 2021; Radnitz and Underwood, 2017; Romer and Jamieson, 2020; Swami, 2012; van Prooijen, 2016). Similarly, present results found that US citizens in our sample with younger age, no college degree, and conservative political leanings reported stronger beliefs in all five conspiracy theories we considered (government malfeasance, malevolent world power, extraterrestrial coverup, personal well-being threat, control of information), and those with Black racial identity reported more beliefs in malevolent world power and personal well-being threat. One interpretation for why conservative study participants reported more conspiracy beliefs of all types may be because at the time our survey was conducted, Democrats controlled the presidency, House of Representatives, and Senate, which may have exaggerated their sense of frustration and powerlessness. One interpretation for why Black study participants reported more mistrust of those in power and threats to their personal well-being may be that at the time of our survey, a number of incidents had occurred in the United States in which White police officers killed unarmed Black individuals (e.g., George Floyd, Breonna Taylor), prompting worldwide protests against racism by the Black Lives Matter movement.

In answer to the question of *WHY?* individuals adopt conspiracy beliefs and violent ideation, past research suggests that individuals may turn to extreme beliefs and behavior when they experience intense psychological distress and/

or feelings of powerlessness (Abalakina-Paap, Stephan, Craig, & Gregory, 1999; Green & Douglas, 2018; Grzesiak-Feldman, 2013; Newheiser, Farias, & Tausch, 2011; Pratt, 2003; Radnitz & Underwood, 2017; Zarefsky, 2014), Similarly, when the US citizens in the present study experienced severe life stressors (health, money, loneliness), especially when in combination with the powerlessness of PTSD symptoms, they were at increased risk for all five of the conspiracy beliefs we evaluated, as well as for willingness to commit violence against others when threatened. Based on principles of the threat appraisal and coping theory (Lazarus and Folkman, 1984), we interpret conspiracy beliefs as a form of "cognitive coping," which may give the individual an improved sense of understanding, strength, and connectedness to others with similar viewpoints. Based on past research showing that violent ideation gives individuals a sense of energy, power, and blamelessness (Herrero, Gadea, Rodríguez-Alarcón, Espert, & Salvador, 2010; Kazén, Kuenne, Frankenberg, & Quirin, 2012), we see it as another cognitive coping mechanism activated when individuals experience severe life stressors and powerlessness. Thus, our answer for *WHY?* individuals adopt conspiracy beliefs and violent ideation may be summarized as a three-step process: *life stressors → PTSD → extreme beliefs as coping behavior.*

Results from the present study may be useful for concerned family members, mental health professionals, and individuals themselves to identify demographic (*WHO?*) and psychological characteristics (*WHY?*) most predictive of extreme beliefs. Present results also suggest three intervention targets to reduce extreme beliefs: demographics, life stressors, PTSD.

EXTREME BELIEF INTERVENTIONS
THAT TARGET DEMOGRAPHICS

Because of the consistent finding of the three-variable sequence (*life stressors → PTSD → extreme beliefs*), one approach for reducing the risk of extreme beliefs would be development of interventions that target modifiable demographics. For example, *low income* was associated with all three life stressors considered in the present study, and *no college* was associated with all five conspiracy beliefs evaluated, which suggests that the risk of extreme beliefs could be reduced with interventions that increase access to college and improved income security. Such interventions might include increased and well-publicized access to free or low-cost community college, jobs training programs, business start-up workshops, business mentorship programs, money-saving and investment training, home-purchase workshops, and community-based cooperative businesses, car-pooling, food supply, and home-repair services. Note: Outright *gifts* of additional income could backfire and result in more PTSD powerlessness or extreme beliefs if individuals perceive themselves as less self-sufficient and capable of solving their life stressors on their own. Another demographic characteristic found associated with PTSD powerlessness symptoms and all five conspiracy beliefs was *social media.* Perhaps the harmful impact of social media could be reduced by public service announcements and personal stories by respected personalities (such as from politics, sports, movies, television, music, science) to educate US citizens about the risks of excessive daily hours on their social media platforms, or that profile alternative activities to bond with their family and friends. Finally, although the less modifiable demographics of younger age and conservative political perspectives were also found associated with PTSD and all five conspiracy beliefs, these demographics may simply assist in identifying individuals at greatest need for interventions to reduce the three-variable sequence toward conspiracy beliefs and violent ideation.

EXTREME BELIEF INTERVENTIONS
THAT TARGET LIFE STRESSORS

Another approach for reducing the risk of extreme beliefs would be development of interventions that target life stressors that appear to start the three-variable sequence (*life stressors → PTSD → extreme beliefs*). For the present study's sample of US citizens, all three life stressors considered (health, money, loneliness) served as significant predictors of PTSD symptoms, and when especially when experienced in combination with PTSD symptoms, they were each linked with increased reports of all five conspiracy beliefs and violent ideation. For example, interventions to reduce health stressors for US citizens could include programs to reduce the cost of expensive medications and surgeries, local and low cost and online access to medical advice, and public service workshops to guide individuals in healthy habits of diet, exercise, and sleep. Additionally, interventions to reduce money stressors could include programs (specified earlier) to improve the individual's income opportunities and money-management strategies. Finally, interventions to reduce loneliness stressors could include creative social support opportunities that focus on shared activities other than social media platforms, which research suggests may provide social support and information, but which can also prompt low self-esteem (Keating, Can, & Hendy, 2016). Seeking social support from trustworthy, caring, and knowledgeable others may reduce health, money, and loneliness stressors (Cox, Owen, & Ogrodniczuk, 2017; Lackner, Brasel, Quigley, Keefer, Krasner, Powell et al., 2010; Shishehgar, Mahmoodi, Dolatian, Mahmoodi, Bakhtiary, & Alavi Majd, 2013). Other ways to achieve a sense of belonging might include social activities in sports or exercise groups, shared meals, enjoyment of nature, artistic and creative pursuits, religious faith, and altruistic volunteering. Past research supports these "healthy coping behaviors" for reduction of anxiety, depression, and loneliness (Goldin, Ziv, Jazaieri, Werner, Kraemer, Heimberg, & Gross, 2012; Smith, Hancock, Blake-Mortimer, & Eckert, 2007; Ulrich-Lai, Christiansen, Ostrander, Jones, Jones, Choi, & McEwen, 2010; Wiborg, Knoop, Stulemeijer, Prins, & Bleijenberg, 2010).

EXTREME BELIEF INTERVENTIONS
THAT TARGET PTSD

Because PTSD symptoms were identified in the present study as a mediator or "link" between each of three life stressors (health, money, loneliness) and each of six extreme beliefs (five conspiracy theories, violent ideation), a final approach to reducing the risk of extreme beliefs and violence would be PTSD interventions. PTSD may be considered a form of *displayed* powerlessness, whether or not the individual has *perceived* powerlessness, because it involves loss of control over a variety of daily functions including sleep, memory, emotions, bodily responses, and social life. One creative approach to PTSD treatment is eye movement desensitization and reprocessing (EMDR), which uses eye stimulation to reduce the intensity of unpleasant repetitive thoughts and emotions by desensitizing the individual's habitual eye movement patterns learned from traumatic experiences (Valiente-Gomez, Moreno-Alcazar, Treen, Cedron, Colom, Perez et al., 2017). Prolonged exposure therapy is a form of cognitive behavioral therapy (CBT) that is often considered the "gold standard" for PTSD treatment (Goldin et al., 2012; Morkved, Hartmann, Aarsheim, Holen, Milde, Bomyea et al., 2014; Wiborg et al., 2010). It guides participants to change their learned thoughts and reactions to anxiety-provoking events by confronting their traumatic memories in a safe space, while developing calmer and more empowered ways to respond to them. Seeking safety is another adaptation of CBT, designed to treat individuals with the comorbid disorders of PTSD and substance use disorder. Seeking safety guides participants to learn safe coping skills across a variety of their interpersonal domains (Najavits, 2002), and it has been an effective and well-received treatment for individuals with PTSD, especially those from vulnerable populations such as prison inmates, military veterans, women exposed to domestic violence, and minorities subject to discrimination (Boden, Kimerling, Jacobs-Lentz, Bowman, Weaver, Carney et al., 2011; Najavitas, 2002).

Two more recent and innovative treatments to reduce PTSD symptoms include transcutaneous vagal nerve stimulation (Lamb, Porges, Lewis, & Williamson, 2017) and psychedelic-assisted therapy (Mitchell, Bogenschutz, Lilienstein, Harrison, Kleiman, Parker-Guilbert et al., 2021). With vagal nerve stimulation, veterans who have comorbid PTSD and traumatic brain injury may reduce their startle responses and anxiety in response to environmental triggers such as being dropped backward and viewing graphic and disturbing images. During psychedelic-assisted therapy, methylenedioxymethamphetamine (MDMA, "ecstasy") is given to PTSD clients in a calm and comfortable environment with a familiar therapist nearby to support them during the experience. Clients report transformative perceptions of being "born again" with a loosening of previous associations between environmental triggers and PTSD symptoms. The mechanism of these effects is believed to be the psychedelic drug's effects on serotonin receptors.

Chapter 19

Study Limitations and Directions for Future Research

One limitation of the present study is that its survey methods only allow conclusions about variable correlations, not cause-effect directions. For example, we believed that principles of the threat appraisal and coping theory (Lazarus & Folkman, 1984) suggested that when individuals experience life stressors to the extent that they develop powerlessness displayed as PTSD symptoms, that this combination of effects would increase their adoption of extreme beliefs such as conspiracy theories and violent ideation to see themselves as more insightful, strong, and connected. Therefore, our mediational analyses examined the three-variable sequence as *life stressors → powerlessness as PTSD → extreme beliefs,* finding them significant for three life stressors (health, money, loneliness) and for six extreme beliefs (five conspiracy theories, violent ideation). However, the three-variable sequence may also be significant in the opposite direction, such as with *government malfeasance → PTSD → loneliness stressors* (indirect effect = .1369, *SE* = .0185, 99 percent CI = .0898 to .1862). Clarification of the temporal order of the three variables could be accomplished by future longitudinal research that examines how life stressors, the appearance of PTSD symptoms, and adoption of extreme beliefs change over time. Additionally, future experimental research could examine whether interventions that reduce life stressors and PTSD symptoms can produce significant reductions in extreme beliefs for individuals who were randomly assigned to an intervention group, in comparison to individuals randomly assigned to an untreated control group.

Another limitation of the present study was that study participants were entirely US citizens. Also, the present sample of US citizens included a high percentage of those with White racial identity (77.9 percent), four-year college degrees (55.7 percent), middle age (mean = 45.08 years), relatively high yearly income (mean = $66,673, with 23.5 percent over $100,000), and reporting liberal political affiliation (57.3 percent). Future research should recruit more diverse samples of participants, including more international participants, to determine whether the present study's pattern of three-variable associations (*life stressors → PTSD → extreme beliefs*) continues to be found. The present study's finding that none of seven demographic variables considered (age, gender, race, college, income, social media, conservatism) was a significant moderator of this three-variable pattern suggests that it may be widespread, but future research should confirm it with more diverse samples.

Additionally, although the present study evaluated a wide range of thirteen demographic characteristics for their associations with life stressors, PTSD symptoms, and extreme beliefs (age, gender, racial identity, Latino ethnic identity, college education, full-time employment, yearly income, partner status, household others, social media exposure, military experience, regional environment, conservative political affiliation), other demographics may have had effects on our primary study variables. Future research could add consideration of the impact of religiosity (Marques, Ling, Williams, Kerr, & McLennan, 2022; Routledge, Abeyta, & Roylance, 2017), community involvement, children and other dependents, and health-related variables (such as past COVID-19 infection, weight status, diet, alcohol consumption, exercise). Many of these variables could influence the severity of life stressors and PTSD symptoms as experienced by US citizens, and therefore effect how likely they are to adopt extreme beliefs as coping behaviors rather than more healthful alternatives (social support, exposure to nature, creative pursuits, altruism).

Future research could also examine whether the three-variable sequence found significant in the present study for *general* conspiracy beliefs as the outcome variable (*life stressors → PTSD → extreme beliefs*) would also be significant for more *specific* conspiracy beliefs such as QAnon, Anti-Vaxx, Holocaust denial, moon landing denial, and Stop the Steal. We used general descriptions of conspiracy beliefs in the present study rather than such specific beliefs to avoid triggering angry rejection of our survey by potential study participants in case they held strong views about these specific beliefs. However, we propose that a focus on specific beliefs would reveal the same three-variable sequence found so consistently in the present study for five conspiracy beliefs (government malfeasance, malevolent world power, extra-terrestrial coverup, personal well-being threat, control of information) and for violent ideation. In the present study's sample of 977 US citizens, all five of these *general* conspiracy beliefs were directly associated with more violent ideation, so another challenge for future research would be to identify *specific* conspiracy beliefs significantly associated with more willingness to commit violence.

Bibliography

37th parliament, 2nd sessions edited hansard; number 110. (2003, June 3) *Parliament of Canada.* https://www.ourcommons.ca/DocumentViewer/en/37-2/house/sitting -110/hansard#Int-579492

60 Minutes investigates the death of Jeffrey Epstein. (2020, January 5). CBS. https:// www.cbsnews.com/news/did-jeffrey-epstein-kill-himself-60-minutes-investigates -2020-01-05

Aaronovitch, D. (2009, April 29). 9/11 conspiracy theories: The truth is out there . . . just not on the internet. *The Times.* London. https://www.thetimes.co.uk/article/911 -conspiracy-theories-the-truth-is-out-therejust-not-on-the-internet-77z7sbxvtxh

Abalakina-Paap, M., Stephan, W. G., Craig, T., & Gregory, W. L. (1999). Beliefs in conspiracies. *Political Psychology, 20,* 637–647. https://doi.org/10.1111/0162 -895X.00160

ABD nin deprem silahı HAARP 17 Ağustos depreminde kullanıldı mı? (in Turkish). (2017, August 17). *Yeni Akit.* https://www.yeniakit.com.tr/haber/abdnin-deprem -silahi-haarp-17-agustos-depreminde-kullanildi-mi-367927.html

Abraham, S., Adorjan, K., Ahmed, H. U., Auwal, S. S., Bjedov, S., Bobes, J., et al. (2022). Results of the COVID-19 mental health international for the general population (COMET-G) study. *European Neuropsychopharmacology, 54,* 21–40. https: //doi.org/10.1016/j.euroneuro.2021.10.004

Agnew, R. (1992). Foundation for a general strain theory of crime and delinquency. *Criminology, 30,* 47–88.

Akyol, M. (2016, September 12). The tin-foil hats are out in Turkey. *Foreign Policy.* https://foreignpolicy.com/2016/09/12/the-tin-foil-hats-are-out-in-turkey/

Albrecht, K. (2010). Microchip-induced tumors in laboratory rodents and dogs: A review of the literature 1990–2006. *IEEE.* pp. 337–349. https://doi.org/10.1109/ ISTAS.2010.5514622

Amadi, K. U., Uwakwe, R., Odinka, P. C., Ndukuba, A. C., Muomah, C. R., & Ohaeri, J. U. (2015). Religion, coping and outcome in outpatients with depression or diabetes mellitus. *Acta Psychiatrica Scandinavica, 133,* 489–496. https://doi.org/10 .1111/acps.12537

Ananth, V. (2020, October 14). The strange, sometimes sinister conspiracy theories on Sushant Singh Rajput's death that flourished on social media. *The Economic*

Times. https://economictimes.indiatimes.com/tech/internet/the-strange-sometimes
-sinister-conspiracy-theories-on-sushant-singh-rajputs-death-that-flourished-on
-social-media/articleshow/78636570.cms

Anderson, G. M. (2008, November 17). Unmasking the truth. *America*. https://www
.americamagazine.org/issue/culture/unmasking-truth

Andone, D., Hartung, K., & Simon, D. (2017, November 6). At least 26 people killed
in shooting at Texas church. CNN. https://www.cnn.com/2017/11/05/us/texas
-church-shooting/index.html

Andrade, G. (2021). Covid-19 vaccine hesitancy, conspiracist beliefs, paranoid ideation and perceived ethnic discrimination in a sample of university students in
Venezuela. *Vaccine, 39,* 6837–6842. https://dx.doi.org/10.1016/j.vaccine.2021.10
.037

Ansari, T. (2017, November 5). Here is the misinformation going around about the
Texas church shooting. *BuzzFeed News*. https://www.buzzfeednews.com/article/
talalansari/fake-news-about-the-texas-church-shooting#.gfb27Rayj

Anthony, A., & Moulding, R. (20192020). Breaking the news: Belief in fake news
and conspiracist beliefs. *Australian Journal of Psychology, 71,* 154–162. https://
doi.org/10.1111/ajpy.12233

Arab media accuse US, Israel of coronavirus conspiracy against China. (2020,
February 909). *The Jerusalem Post*. https://www.jpost.com/Middle-East/Arab
-media-accuse-US-Israel-of-coronavirus-conspiracy-against-China-617021

Arab writers: The coronavirus is part of biological warfare waged by the U.S. against
China. (2020, February 6). *Middle East Media Research Institute*. https://www
.memri.org/reports/arab-writers-coronavirus-part-biological-warfare-waged-US
-against-china

Aronczyk, A. (2021, August 20). *Planet Money* investigates the base rate fallacy as
it pertains to the pandemic. NPR. https://www.npr.org/2021/08/20/1029582399/
planet-money-investigates-the-base-rate-fallacy-as-it-pertains-to-the-pandemic

Arora, P. (2020, June 14). Sushant Singh Rajput, Bollywood star, dies at 34. *The New
York Times*. https://www.nytimes.com/2020/06/14/world/asia/sushant-singh-rajput
-death.html

Assassination Records Review Board, FY 1995 Report, The Record Review Process
and Compliance with the JFK Act. *U.S. Secret Service*. https://sgp.fas.org/advisory
/arrb.html

Austin, J. (2016, August 25). Mark of the beast: Secret plan to implant us all with
ID chips by 2017. *Express*. https://www.express.co.uk/news/weird/703856/MARK
-OF-THE-BEAST-Secret-plan-to-implant-us-all-with-ID-chips-by-2017

Aziken, E. (2011, March 21). 53 suitcases saga: Buhari blasts Atiku, Jonathan.
Vanguard News. https://www.vanguardngr.com/2011/03/53-suitcases-saga-buhari
-blasts-atiku-jonathan

Bacon Jr., P. (2007, November 29). Foes use Obama's Muslim ties to fuel rumors
about him. *The Washington Post*. https://www.washingtonpost.com/wp-dyn/
content/article/2007/11/28/AR2007112802757.html?hpid=topnews

Baenen, J. (2013, December 14). Ventura seeks out conspiracy theories at Alaska station. *Juneau Empire.* https://web.archive.org/web/20131214195544/http://juneauempire.com/stories/120309/sta_531557452.shtml

Baker, J. (2010). *Me and Lee: How I came to know, love and lose Lee Harvey Oswald.* Walterville: Trine Day. p., 150. ISBN 978-0–9799886–7–7.

Barcelona clubbers get chipped. (2004, September 29). *BBC News.* 2004–09–29. http://news.bbc.co.uk/2/hi/technology/3697940.stm

Barkun, M. (2003). A culture of conspiracy: Apocalyptic visions in contemporary America. *Comparative Studies in Religion and Society.* Berkeley: University of California Press. ISBN 978-0–520–23805–3.

Barnitz, K. (2017, November 5). NM court documents detail Devin Kelley's divorce. *Albuquerque Journal.* https://www.abqjournal.com/1088469/nm-court-documents-detail-devin-kelleys-divorce

Barron, D., Morgan, K., Towell, T., Altemeyer, B., & Swami, V. (2014). Associations between schizotypy and belief in conspiracist ideation. *Personality and Individual Differences, 70,* 156–159. https://doi.org/10.1016/j.paid.2014.06.040]

Bartleet, L. (2017, May 16). Imposter alert! Nine ridiculous conspiracy theories about celebrity changelings. *NME.* https://www.nme.com/blogs/nme-blogs/celebrity-imposter-theory-clone-miley-2072581.

Bathembu, C. (2009, October 18). Zuma appoints new Public Protector. *SA News.* https://www.sanews.gov.za/south-africa/zuma-appoints-new-public-protector

Baur, J. (2021, February 17). Anti-Semitic flyer in German tram blames Jews for COVID pandemic. *Jewish Telegraphic Agency.* https://www.jta.org/quick-reads/anti-semitic-flyer-in-german-tram-blames-jews-for-the-covid-pandemic

Berger, R., & Tiry, M. (2012). The enchanting forest and the healing sand: Nature therapy with people coping with psychiatric difficulties. *The Arts in Psychotherapy, 39,* 412–416 https://doi.org/10.1016/j.aip.2012.03.009.

Bergland, A., Thorsen, K., & Loland, N. W. (2010). The relationship between coping, self-esteem and health on outdoor walking ability among older adults in Norway. *Aging and Society, 30,* 949–963. https://doi.org/10.1017/S0144686X1000022X

Berlet, C., & Lyons, M. N. (2000). *Right-wing populism in America: Too close for comfort.* Guilford Press.

Biddlestone, M., Green, R., & Douglas, K. M. (2020). Cultural orientation, power, belief in conspiracy theories, and intentions to reduce the spread of COVID-19. *British Journal of Social Psychology,* 59, 663–673. https://doi.org/10.1111/bjso.12397

Biello, D. (2010, February 1). Negating "Climategate." *Scientific American,. (302),:2.16.* ISSN 0036–8733.

Bischoff, L.A. (2021, June 9). GOP-invited Ohio doctor Sherri Tenpenny falsely tells Ohio lawmakers COVID-19 shots "magnetize" people, create 5G "interfaces.." *The Columbus Dispatch.* https://www.msn.com/en-us/news/us/gop-invited-ohio-doctor-sherri-tenpenny-falsely-tells-ohio-lawmakers-Covid-19-shots-magnetize-people-create-5g-interfaces/ar-AAKS8aM

Black, P. (2018). *Minorities and deviance: Coping strategies of the power-poor.* Lanham, MD: Lexington Books.

Black, P., & Hendy, H. M. (2018). Perceived powerlessness as a mediator between life stressors and deviant behaviors. *Deviant Behavior, 40,* 1080–1089. https://doi .org/10.1080/01639625.2018.1461744

Blatchford, A. (2010, April 30). U.S. skeptics to speak of 9–11 cover-up at three Canadian universities. *Toronto Star.* https://www.thestar.com/news/canada/2010 /04/30/us_skeptics_to_speak_of_911_coverup_at_three_canadian_universities .html

Blount, B. K. (2009). *Revelation: A commentary.* Louisville, Kentucky: Westminster Knox Press. pp., 248–249. ISBN 978-0-664-22121-8

Boden, M. T., Kimerling, R., Jacobs-Lentz, J., Bowman, D., Weaver, C., Carney, D., et al. (2011). Seeking Safety safety treatment for male veterans with a substance use disorder and post-traumatic stress disorder symptomatology. *Addiction, 107,* 578–586. https://doi.org/10.1111/j.1360-0443.2011.03658.x

Brotherton, R., French, C. C., & Pickering, A. D. (2013). Measuring belief in conspiracy theories: The Generic Conspiracist Beliefs Scale. *Frontiers in Psychology, 21.* https://doi.org/10.3389/fpsyg.2013.00279

Budge, S. L., Adelson, J. L., & Howard, K. A. S. (2013). Anxiety and depression in transgender individuals: The roles of transition status, loss, social support, and coping. *Journal of Consulting and Clinical Psychology, 81,* 545–557. https://doi .org/10.1037/a0031774

Dunson, M. (2009). *Encyclopedia of the Roman Empire.* Infobase Publishing. ISBN 978-1-4381- 1027–1.

Buss, A. H., & Perry, M. (1992). The Aggression Questionnaire. *Journal of Personality and Social Psychology, 63,* 452–459. https://doi.org/10.1037/0022 -3514.63.3.452

Buturoiu, R., Udrea, G., Oprea, D., & Corbu, N. (2021). Who believes in conspiracy theories about the COVID-19 pandemic in Romania? an An analysis of conspiracy theories believers' profiles. *Societies* (Basel, Switzerland), *11*(4), 138. https://doi .org/10.3390/soc11040138

Byrne, B. P. (2017, August 28). Minecraft creator alleges global conspiracy Involving involving Pizzagate, a "manufactured race war," a missing tabloid toddler, and holistic medicine." *The Daily Beast.* https://www.thedailybeast.com/minecraft -creator-alleges-global-conspiracy-involving-pizzagate-a-manufactured-race-war -a-missing-tabloid-toddler-and-holistic-medicine

Camero, K. (2021, June 7). No, COVID vaccines don't make you magnetic. Experts debunk social media videos. *Idaho Statesman.* https://www.idahostatesman.com/ news/coronavirus/article251955083.html

Camlibel, D. A., Can, S. H., & Hendy, H. M. (2021). Predictors of violence reported by female and male inmates in Wisconsin State Prisons. *Women and Criminal Justice, 31,* 505–517. https://doi.org/10.1080/08974454.2021.1892565

Cardona, A.C. (2020, March 11). Leaked emails: Norwegian pressures sales team to mislead potential customers about coronavirus." *Miami New Times.* https:// www.miaminewtimes.com/news/coronavirus-norwegian-cruise-line-leaked-emails -show-booking-strategy-11590056

Carey, J. M. (2019). Who believes in conspiracy theories in Venezuela? *Latin American Research Review, 54,* 444–457. https://doi.org/10.25222/larr.88

Carlson, T. (2020, November 11). Tucker Carlson: Yes, dead people voted in this election and Democrats helped make it happen. *Fox News.* https://www.foxnews.com/opinion/tucker-carlson-2020-presidential-election-voter-fraud-dead-voters

Carroll, L. (2017, May 23). The baseless claim that slain DNC staffer Seth Rich gave emails to WikiLeaks. *PolitiFact.* https://www.politifact.com/factchecks/2017/may/23/newt-gingrich/claim-slain-dnc-staffer-seth-rich-gave-emails-wiki/

Chalfant, M. (2020, March 4). Trump says Biden Ukraine dealings will be a "major" campaign issue. *The Hill.* https://thehill.com/homenews/campaign/486054-trump-says-Biden-Ukraine-dealings-will-be-a-major-campaign-issue/

Chandler, A. (2015, February 13). The Pope Benedict Conspiracy conspiracy Theoriestheories. *The Atlantic.* https://www.theatlantic.com/international/archive/2015/02/Pope-Benedict-XVI-resignation-forced-conspiracy-theory/385462/

Chen, Y., & Feeley, T. H. (2014). Social support, social strain, loneliness, and well-being among older adults: An analysis of the health and retirement study. *Journal of Social and Personal Relationships, 31,* 141–161. https://doi.org/10.1177/0265407513488728

China coronavirus: Misinformation spreads online about origin and scale. (January 30, 2020). BBC News. https://www.bbc.com/news/blogs-trending-51271037

China's rulers see the coronavirus as a chance to tighten their grip. (2020, February 8). *The Economist.* https://www.economist.com/china/2020/02/08/chinas-rulers-see-the-coronavirus-as-a-chance-to-tighten-their-grip

Cloward, T. (2013). Conspiracy-a-go-go: Dallas at the fiftieth anniversary of the assassination. *Southwest Review, 98,* 407–436.

Cohen, L. (2021, January 15). 6 conspiracy theories about the 2020 election-debunked. CBS News. https://www.bing.com/search?q=6+conspiracy+theories+about+the+2020+election-debunked

Collins, B., & Alba, M. (2019, July 11). Conspiracy theorists, far-right agitators head to White House with social media in their sights. NBC. https://www.nbcnews.com/tech/social-media/conspiracy-theorists-far-right-agitators-head-white-house-social-media-n1028576

Collins, D. (2014, March 24). FBI to Quiz quiz Wife wife of MH370 pilot amid talk of cockpit hijack. *Mirror.* https://www.mirror.co.uk/news/world-news/missing-malaysia-airlines-flight-fbi-3276536

Collins, P., & Swalec, A. (2016, July 11). 27-Yearyear-Old old DNC Staffer staffer Seth Rich Shotshot, Killed killed in Northwest DC. *NBC Washington.* https://www.nbcwashington.com/news/local/man-shot-killed-in-northwest-dc/2074048/

Collins, S. (2021, September 11). 9 stars who have been 9/11 conspiracy truthers. MSN. https://www.msn.com/en-us/movies/news/9-stars-who-have-been-9-11-conspiracy-truthers-photos/ss-BB18W2R4

Company overview of Dominion Voting Systems Corporation. (2017, June 21). *Bloomberg.* https://www.bloomberg.com/profile/company/1045239D:US

Connelly, E. (2020, November 7). Falsely accused election worker in viral video forced to go into hiding. *New York Post*. https://nypost.com/2020/11/07/falsely -accused-election-worker-forced-to-go-into-hiding/

Cookson, D., Jolley, D., Dempsey, R. C., & Povey, R. (2021). "If they believe, then so shall I": Perceived beliefs of the in-group predict conspiracy theory belief. *Group Processes and Intergroup Relations, 24,* 759–782. https://doi.org/10.1177 /1368430221993907

Cooper, J. (2021, June 2). Arizona GOP election audit draws more Republican politicians. *ABC News*. https://abcnews.go.com/Politics/wireStory/arizona-gop -election- audit-draws-republican-politicians-7803390

Corasaniti, N., Epstein, R., & Rutenberg, J. (2020, November 10). The *Times* called officials in every state: No evidence of voter fraud. *The New York Times*. https:// www.nytimes.com/2020/11/10/us/politics/voting-fraud.html

Coronavirus death toll climbs in China, and a lockdown widens. (2020, January 23). *The New York Times*. https://www.nytimes.com/2020/01/23/world/asia/china -coronavirus.html

Covid-19 Dashboard by the Center for Systems Science and Engineering (CSSE) at Johns Hopkins University. *Johns Hopkins University*. https://systems.jhu.edu/ research/public-health/ncov/

Covid-19 found in semen of infected men, say Chinese doctors. (2020, May 7). *The Guardian*. https://www.theguardian.com/world/2020/may/07/Covid-19-found-in -semen-of-infected-men-say-chinese-doctors

Cox, D. W., Owen, J. J., & Ogrodniczuk, J. S. (2017). Group psychotherapeutic factors and perceived social support among veterans with PTSD symptoms. *Journal of Nervous and Mental Disease, 205,* 127–132. https://doi.org/10.1097/NMD .0000000000000635

Crellin, Z. (2020, March 9). Sorry to the French people who thought cocaine would protect them from coronavirus. *Pedestrian*. https://www.pedestrian.tv/news /french- government-cocaine-coke-coronavirus-hoax/

Crocker, J., Luhtanen, R., Broadnax, S., & Blaine, B. E. (1999). Belief in U.S. government conspiracies against blacks Blacks among black and white college students: Powerlessness or system blame? *Personality and Social Psychology Bulletin, 25,* 941–953. https://doi.org/10.1177/01461672992511003

Cryer, N. B. (2006). *York Mysteries mysteries Revealedrevealed. (Understanding understanding an Old English Masonic Traditiontradition)*. Chilton Books.

Danforth, N. (2014, October 2). Notes on a Turkish conspiracy. *Foreign Policy*. https: //foreignpolicy.com/2014/10/02/notes-on-a-turkish-conspiracy/

Daniels, T. (2015, May 11). "Brady Suspended 4 games, Patriots lose draft picks. *The Bleacher Report*. https://bleacherreport.com/articles/2458473-tom-brady -deflategate-latest-news-and-rumors-on-qbs-potential-punishment

Datta P. (2020, April 6). Coronavirus outbreak sparks racist attacks on people from North East, stokes Islamophobia on social media. *Firstpost*. https://www.firstpost .com/health/coronavirus-outbreak-sparks-racist-attacks-on-people-from-north-east -stokes-islamophobia-on-social-media-8231371.html

Davies, G. (2018, December 3) Nigeria's President president denies conspiracy theories that he's a human clone. Abcnews.go.com. https://abcnews.go.com/ International/nigerias-president-denies-conspiracy-theories-human-clone/story?id =59574279

Davis, J., Wetherell, G. and Henry, P. (2018), Social devaluation of African Americans and race- related conspiracy theories. *European Journal of Social Psychology, 48,* 999–1010. https://doi-org.ezaccess.libraries.psu.edu/10.1002/ejsp.2531

de Vos, P. (2014, July 9). Wishful thinking: If the public protector were helped to do her job. *Daily Maverick.* https://www.dailymaverick.co.za/opinionista/2014-07-09 -wishful-thinking-if-the-public-protector-were-helped-to-do-her-job/

Dean, S. (2006, April 10). Physicist says heat substance felled WTC. *Deseret Morning News.* https://www.deseret.com/2006/4/10/19947618/physicist-says-heat -substance-felled-wtc

Donovan, B. W. (2011, July 20). *Conspiracy films. A tour of dark places in the American conscious.* McFarland. ISBN 978–0786486151

dos Santos, A. T., Soares, F. C., Lima, R. A., dos Santos, S. J., Silva, Bezerra, C. R. M., & Garros, M. V. G. (2021). Violence and psychosocial stress: A 10-year time trend analysis. *Journal of Affective Disorders, 295,* 116–122. https://doi.org/10 .1016/j.jad.2021.08.011

Douglas, K. M., & Sutton, R. M. (2015, March 1). Climate change: Why the conspiracy theories are dangerous. *Bulletin of the Atomic Scientists, 71,* 98—106.. https:// doi:10.1177/0096340215571908

Douglas, K.M., Uscinski, J.E., Sutton, R.M., Cichocka, A., Nefes, T., Ang, C.S. ad & Deravi, F. (2019),). Understanding conspiracy theories. *Political Psychology, 40,* 3–35. https://doi-org.ezaccess.libraries.psu.edu/10.1111/pops.1256

Dow, B. J., Johnson, A. L., Wang, C. S., Whitson, J., & Menon, T. (2021). The Covid-19 pandemic and the search for structure: Social media and conspiracy theories. *Social and Personality Psychology Compass, 15,* e12636. https://doi.org /10.1111/spc3.12636

Drobnic Holan, A., Kertscher, T. & Sherman, A. (2021, June 14). Donald Trump's "I was right about everything," fact-checked. *PolitiFact.* https://www.politifact.com/ article/2021/Jun/14/donald-trumps-I-was-right-about-everything-fact-ch/

Dubay, E. (2014). *The Flat-Earth Conspiracy.* Lulu.com. ISBN 978–1312627161.

Duke, A. (2014, March 26). Investigators: Speed——not drugs, racing or mechanical failure– –killed Paul Walker. CNN. https://www.cnn.com/2014/03/25/showbiz/ paul-walker-crash-probe/index.html

Duke, A., & Sutton, J. (2013, November 30). "Fast & Furious" star Paul Walker killed in car crash. CNN. https://www.cnn.com/2013/11/30/showbiz/actor-paul-walker -dies/

Durkheim, E. (1897). *Suicide: A Study of Sociology.* 1st ed. Paris.

Dyrendal, A., Kennair, L. E. O., & Bendixen, M. (2021). Predictors of belief in conspiracy theory: The role of individual differences in schizotypal traits, paranormal beliefs, social dominance orientation, right wing authoritarianism and conspiracy mentality. *Personality and Individual Differences, 173,* e110645. https://doi.org/10 .1016/j.paid.2021.110645

Estatie, L. (2017, May 15). The Avril Lavigne conspiracy theory returns. *BBC News*. https://www.bbc.com/news/blogs-trending-39921209

Evans, S. (2021, February 16). Zondo vs. Zuma explained. *Explain*. https://explain.co .za/2021/02/16/zondo-vs-zuma-explained/

Evon, D. (2015, November 5). Conspiracy weary. *Snopes*. https://www.snopes.com/ fact-check/avril-lavigne-dead-conspiracy-theory/

Evon, D. (2021, November 2). "Luciferase" is not an ingredient in Covid-19 vaccines. *Snopes.com*. https://www.snopes.com/fact-check/luciferase-Covid -19- vaccines/

Eyal, P., David, R., Andrew, G., Zak, E., & Ekaterina, D. (2021). Data quality of platforms and panels for online behavioral research. *Behavioral Research Methods*. https://doi.org/10.3758/513428-021-01694-3

Factual information, safety investigation: Malaysia Airlines MH370 Boeing 777– 200ER (9M-MRO) (2014, March 8). *Malaysia: Malaysia Ministry of Transport*. https://www.mot.gov.my/en/Laporan%20MH%20370/Interim%20Statement %20Safety%20Investigation%20For%20MH370.pdf

Fandos, N. (2020, September 23). Republican inquiry finds no evidence of wrong-doing by Biden. *The New York Times*. https://www.nytimes.com/2020/09/23/us/ politics/biden-inquiry-republicans-johnson.html

Farley, R. (2020, November 9). Thin allegations of dead people voting. *FactCheck.org*. https://www.factcheck.org/2020/11/thin-allegations-of-dead-people-voting/

Findings. Report of the Select Committee on Assassinations. (2016, August 15). *U.S. House of Representatives*. Vol. 9, p. 336, par. 917. Retrieved April 14, 2022.

Fisher, M.. Cox, J., & Hermann, P. (2016, December 6). Pizzagate: From rumor, to hashtag, to gunfire in D.C. *The Washington Post*. https://www.washingtonpost.com /local/pizzagate-from-rumor-to-hashtag-to-gunfire-in-dc/2016/12/06/4c7def50 -bbd4-11e6-94ac-3d324840106c_story.html

Flynn, M. (2018, March 8). Conspiracy theorists harass Sutherland Springs church-goers, pastor whose daughter was killed. *The Washington Post*. https://www .washingtonpost.com/news/morning-mix/wp/2018/03/08/conspiracy-theorists -harass-sutherland-springs-churchgoers-pastor-whose-daughter-was-killed/

Foa, E. B., Cashman, L., Joycox, L., & Perry, K. (1997). The validation of a self-report measure of posttraumatic stress disorder: The Posttraumatic Diagnostic Scale. *Psychological Assessment, 9*, 445–451. https://doi.org/10.1037/1040-3590.9.4.445

Fraser, S. (2009). Phantom menace? Are conspirators using aircraft to pollute the sky? *Current Science, 94*, 8–9.

Frazier, K. (2010). *The hundredth monkey: And other paradigms of the paranormal*. Prometheus Books, Publishers, ISBN 978-1–61592–401-1.

Frizell, S. (2014, March 11). The missing Malaysian Plane: 5 conspiracy theories. *Time*. https://time.com/20351/missing-plane-flight-mh370-5-conspiracy-theories/

Fuller, T. K., & Schmitt, E. (2014, March 8). Passport theft adds to mystery of missing Malaysia Airlines jet. *The New York Times*. https://www.nytimes.com/2014/03/09/ world/asia/malaysia-airlines-flight.html

Galer, S. (2020, July 11). The accidental invention of the Illuminati conspiracy. *BBC*. https://www.bbc.com/future/article/20170809-the-accidental-invention-of -the-illuminati-conspiracy

Gardner, F., & Fisher, J. (2014, March 15). Missing Malaysia Airlines plane "deliberately diverted.." *BBC News*. https://www.bbc.com/news/world-asia-26591056

Geheimbotschaften in der Jeanshose. (2017, November 27). Der Tagesspiegel. https://www.tagesspiegel.de/politik/verschwoerungstheorie-in-der-tuerkei -geheimbotschaften-in-der-jeanshose/20637406.html

Gillin, J. (2017, November 6). Fake news: No proof Antifa, communism compelled Texas shooter Devin Kelley. *PolitiFact*. https://www.politifact.com/factchecks /2017/nov/06/yournewswirecom/fake-news-no-proof-antifa-communism -compelled-texa/

Goldberg, R. A. (2008), *Enemies within: The culture of conspiracy in modern America*. Yale University Press, p. pp. 189, ISBN 978-0-300-13294-6.

Goldin, P. R., Ziv, M., Jazaieri, H., Werner, K., Kraemer, H., Heimberg, R. G., & Gross, J. J. (2012). Cognitive reappraisal self-efficacy mediates the effects of individual cognitive-behavioral therapy for social anxiety disorder. *Journal of Consulting and Clinical Psychology, 80*, 1034–1040. https://doi.org/10.1037/ a0028555

Goreis, A., & Voracek, M. (2019). A systematic review and meta-analysis of psychological research on conspiracy beliefs. *Frontiers in Psychology, 11*. https://doi.org /10.3389/fpsyg.2019.00205

Graff, G. M. (2017, September 3). The secret history of FEMA. *Wired*. https://www .wired.com/story/the-secret-history-of-fema/

Green, R., & Douglas, K. M. (2018). Anxious attachment and belief in conspiracy theories. *Personality and Individual Differences*, *125,* 30–37.

Gregory, J. (September 13, 2021). The top COVID-19 vaccine myths spreading online. *NewsGuard*. https://www.newsguardtech.com/special-reports/special -report-top-Covid-19-vaccine-myths/

Griffin, A. (2017, November 6). Texas shooting: US far-right try to spread conspiracy theories about motive behind church murders. *The Independent*. https: //www.independent.co.uk/tech/texas-shooting-conspiracy-theories-us-far-right -sutherland-spring-murders-motive-name-of-killer-gunman-guns-a8039611.html

Gross, T. (2007, Nov. 9). Weather Channel boss calls global warming "the greatest scam in history." *National Review*. https://www.nationalreview.com/media-blog/ weather-channel-boss-calls-global-warming-greatest-scam-history-tom-gross/

Grzesiak-Feldman, M. (2013). The effect of high-anxiety situations on conspiracy thinking. *Current Psychology, 32,* 100–118. https://doi.org/10.1007/s12144-013 -9165-6

Gulf of Mexico oil leak "worst US environment disaster.." (2020, May 30). *BBC News*. https://www.bbc.com/news/10194335

Guo, J. (2017, May 24). The bonkers Seth Rich conspiracy theory, explained. *Vox*. https://www.vox.com/policy-and-politics/2017/5/24/15685560/seth-rich -conspiracy-theory-explained-fox-news-hannity

Hammell, K. (2006). *Perspectives on disability and rehabilitation: Contesting assumptions, challenging practice*. New York: Churchill Livingstone.

Hancke, G. P. (2011). Practical eavesdropping and skimming attacks on high-frequency RFID tokens. *Journal of Computer Security, 19*, 259–288.

Hanson, M. (2019, July 20). Celebrities who envy deny the moon landing and other idiots. *Popdust*. https://www.popdust.com/celebrity-moon-landing-denier -2639280416.html

Hartley, L., Fleay, C., & Tye, M. E. (2017). Exploring physical activity engagement and barriers for asylum seekers in Australia coping with prolonged uncertainty and no right to work. *Health and Social Care in the Community, 25*, 1190–1198. https: //doi.org/10.1111/hsc.12419

Harwell, D. (2020, December 1). To boost voter-fraud claims Trump Advocate advocate Sidney Powell turns to unusual source: The longtime operator of QAnon's internet home. *The Washington Post*. https://www.washingtonpost.com/technology /2020/12/01/powell-cites-qanon-watkins/

Haven, L. (2014, July 19). Global elite take down Malaysian Airline MH17 to hide the cure for Aids? Getting rid of the cure to keep money in their pockets and continue their depopulation agenda. *Before It's News*. https://beforeitsnews.com/power -elite/2014/07/illuminati-takes-down-malaysian-airline-mh17-to-hide-the-cure-for -aids-getting-rid-of-the-cure-to-keep-money-in-their-pockets-and-continue-their -depopulation-agenda-2446354.html

Heen, M. S. J., Lieberman, J. D., & Miethe, T. D. (2014). A comparison of differing online sampling approaches for generating national samples. *Center for Crime and Justice Policy*. https://www.unlv.edu/sites/default/files/page_files/27/Comparison DifferentOnlineSampling.pdf

Heiss, R., Gell, S., Röthlingshöfer, E., & Zoller, C. (2021). How threat perceptions relate to learning and conspiracy beliefs about COVID-19: Evidence from a panel study. *Personality and Individual Differences, 175*, 110672–110672. https://doi.org /10.1016/j.paid.2021.110672

Hendy, H. M., Black, P., Can, S. H., Fleischut, A., & Aksen, D. (2018). Opioid abuse as maladaptive coping to life stressors in U.S. adults. *Journal of Drug Issues, 48*, 560–571. https://doi.org/10.1177/0022042618783454

Henley, J. (2002, April 1). US invented air attack on Pentagon, claims French book. *The Guardian*. https://www.theguardian.com/world/2002/apr/01/september11.france

Herrero, N., Gadea, M., Rodríguez-Alarcón, G., Espert, R., & Salvador, A. (2010). What happens when we get angry? Hormonal, cardiovascular and asymmetrical brain responses. *Hormones and Behavior, 3*, 276–283. https://doi.org/10.1016/j .yhbeh.2009.12.008

Hettich, N., Beutel, M. E., Ernst, M., Schliessler, C., Kampling, H., Kruse, J., & Braehler, E. (2022). Conspiracy endorsement and its associations with personality functioning, anxiety, loneliness, and sociodemographic characteristics during the COVID-19 pandemic in a representative sample of the German population. *PloS One, 17*, e0263301–e0263301. https://doi.org/10.1371/journal.pone.0263301

Hinkelman, M. (2008, October 25). Judge rejects Montco lawyer's bid to have Obama removed from ballot. *The Philadelphia Daily News*. https://freerepublic.com/focus /f-news/2114883/posts

Hiroto, D. S., & Seligman, M. E. (1975). Generality of learned helplessness in man. *Journal of Personality and Social Psychology, 31*, 311–327. https://doi.org/10 .1037/h0076270

Hitt, T. (2020, August 14). How QAnon became obsessed With "adrenochrome," an imaginary drug Hollywood is "harvesting" from kids. *The Daily Beast*. https: //www.thedailybeast.com/how-qanon-became-obsessed-with-adrenochrome-an -imaginary-drug-hollywood-is-harvesting-from-kids/

Hodapp, C. L., and & Von Kannon, A. (2008). *Conspiracy theories & secret societies for dummies*. Wiley, ISBN 978-0–470–18408–0.

Holan, A. (2007, December 20). Obama sworn in on his Bible. *PolitiFact*. https:// www.politifact.com/factchecks/2007/dec/20/chain-email/obama-sworn-in-on-his -bible/

Holland, M. (2004, April 5). The British JFK producer who brought shame on the History Channel. *History News Network*. https://historynewsnetwork.org/article /4487

Hollyfield, A. (2008, April 2). Obama is the antichrist? Puh-leeze!. *Politifact*. https:// www.politifact.com/article/2008/apr/02/barack-obama-not-antichrist/

Houston M. (2020, May 17). More athletes claim they contracted COVID-19 at Military World Games in Wuhan. *Inside the Games*. https://www.insidethegames .biz/articles/1094347/world-military-games-illness-Covid-19

Hovannisian, R. (2015). Denial of the Armenian genocide 100 years later: The new practitioners and their trade. *Genocide Studies International, 9*, 228–247. https:// doi.org/10.3138/gsi.9.2.04

Hunter, M. (1978, December 31). House panel reports a conspiracy "probable" in the Kennedy slaying. *The New York Times*. https://www.nytimes.com/1978/12/31 /archives/house-panel-reports-a-conspiracy-probable-in-the-kennedy-slaying.html

Hyde, M. (2017, October 19). Who started the "Melania Trump body double" conspiracy theory? Look no further. *The Guardian*. https://www.theguardian.com /lifeandstyle/lostinshowbiz/2017/oct/19/who-started-melania-trump-body-double -conspiracy-theory

Iran cleric blames Trump for coronavirus outbreak in religious city. (2020, February 22) *Radio Farda*. https://en.radiofarda.com/a/iran-cleric-blames-trump-for -coronavirus-outbreak-in-religious-city/30449087.html

Isachenkov, V. (2019, September 27). Ukraine's prosecutor says there is no probe into Biden. *PBS Newshour*. https://www.pbs.org/newshour/politics/ukraines-prosecutor -says-there-is-no-probe-into-biden

Ivanov, D., & Dolgui, A. (2020). Viability of intertwined supply networks: Extending the supply chain resilience angles towards survivability. A position paper motivated by COVID-19 outbreak. *International Journal of Production Research, 58*(10), 2904-2915. https://doi.org/10.1080/00207543.2020.1750727

Ivanova, P. (2019, October 19). What Hunter Biden did on the board of Ukrainian energy company Burisma. *Reuters*. https://www.reuters.com/article/us-hunter -biden-ukraine-idUSKBN1WX1P7

Jack the Ripper was a Freemason committing ritualistic murders. (n.d.). The Conspiracy Blog. https://theconspiracyblog.com/conspiracies/secret-societies/ freemasons/1060-jack-the-ripper-was-a-freemason-committing-ritualistic-murders

Jackson, E. M. (2013). Stress relief: The role of exercise in stress management. *Health and Fitness Journal, 17,* 14–19. https://doi.org/10.1249/FIT.0b013e31828cb1c9

Jamieson, A. (2018, October 6). Trump's lawyer retweeted that 'anti"anti-christ' christ" George Soros is funding anti-Kavanaugh protests." *Buzzfeed News*. https:// www.buzzfeednews.com/article/amberjamieson/giuliani-twitter-soros

Janos, A. (2020, September 8). How United Flight 93 passengers fought back on 9/11. *History*. https://www.history.com/news/united-flight-93-september-11 -passengers-revolt-crash

Jansen, B. (2013, July 25). Crash investigators trace UPS plane fire to batteries. *USA Today*. https://www.usatoday.com/story/news/nation/2013/07/24/ups-crash-dubai -lithium/2582213/#:~:text=Crash%20investigators%20in%20the%20United %20Arab%20Emirates%20traced,the%20crew%2C%20according%20to%20a %20report%20released%20Wednesday

Jardina, A., & Traugott, M. (2019). The genesis of the Birther birther rumor: Partisanship, racial attitudes, and political knowledge. *Journal of Race, Ethnicity and Politics, 4,* 60–80. https://doi.org/10.1017/rep.2018.25

Joesten, J. (2013). *The Dark dark Side side of Lyndon Baines Johnson*. Iconoclassic Books. ISBN: 978-1-77152-007-2.

John, A. (2013, October 14) Breaking down the Malala conspiracy theories *The Atlantic*. https://www.theatlantic.com/international/archive/2013/10/breaking -down-malala-conspiracy-theories/309985/

Jolley, D., & Douglas, K. M. (20142013). The social consequences of conspiracism: Exposure to conspiracy theories decreases intentions to engage in politics and to reduce one's carbon footprint. *The British Journal of Psychology, 105,* 35–56. https://doi.org/10.1111/bjop.12018

Jolly, B (2020, February 3). Coronavirus: British man who caught virus "beat flu with glass of hot whisky.." *The Mirror*. https://www.mirror.co.uk/news/uk-news/ coronavirus-first-brit-who-caught-21418662

Kamm, O. (2014, December 11). " "Respectable" revisionists. *The Jewish Chronicle*. https://www.thejc.com/comment/opinion/respectable-revisionists-1.63523

Kang, C. (2016, November 21). Fake News news onslaught targets pizzeria as nest of child- trafficking. *The New York Times*. https://www.nytimes.com/2016/11/21/ technology/fact-check-this-pizzeria-is-not-a-child-trafficking-site.htm

Kang, C., & Goldman, A. (2016, December 5). In Washington pizzeria attack, fake news brought real guns. *The New York Times*. https://www.nytimes.com/2016 /12/05/business/media/comet-ping-pong-pizza-shooting-fake-news-consequences .html

Kasprak, A. (2020, February 24). Do sulfur emissions from Wuhan, China, point to mass cremation of coronavirus victims?. *Snopes*. https://www.snopes.com/fact-check/sulfur-coronavirus-cremations/

Kaysing, B. (2002). [First published 1976]. *We never went to the moon: America's thirty billion dollar swindle*. Randy Reid credited as co-author in 1976 editions. Pomeroy, WA: Health Research Books. OCLC 52390067.

Kazén, M., Kuenne, T., Frankenberg, H., & Quirin, M. (2012). Inverse relation between cortisol and anger and their relation to performance and explicit memory. *Biological Psychology, 2,* 28–35. https://doi.org/10.1016/j.biopsycho.2012.05.006

Keating, R., Can, S. H., & Hendy, H. M. (2016). Demographic and psychosocial variables associated with perceived benefits and costs of using social media. *Computers in Human Behavior, 57,* 93–98. https://doi.org/10.1016/j.chb.2015.12.002

Keller, L. (2010, March 30). Fear of FEMA.. *Southern Poverty Law Center*. https://www.splcenter.org/fighting-hate/intelligence-report/2010/fear-fema.

Kertschner, T. (2021, October 29). No evidence that Pfizer Covid-19 vaccine causes blood clots. *PolitiFact*. https://www.politifact.com/factchecks/2021/oct/29/instagram-posts/no-evidence-pfizer-Covid-19-vaccine-causes-blood-c/

Kiely, E. (2017, May 22). Gingrich spreads conspiracy theory. *FactCheck*. https://www.factcheck.org/2017/05/gingrich-spreads-conspiracy-theory/

Klepper, D., & Swenson, A. (2022, May 26, 2022). '"Horrifying' conspiracy theories swirl around Texas shooting. *AP News*. https://apnews.com/article/uvalde-school-shooting-government-and-politics-shootings-texas-conspiracy-theories-8d9ac3b6 1420c6542b11d0da3f0b3a16.

Klonoff, E. A., & Landrine, H. (1999). Do Blacks believe that HIV/AIDS is a government conspiracy against them? *Preventive Medicine, 28*, 451–457. https://doi.org/10.1006/pmed.1999.0463

Knight, P. (2003), *Conspiracy theories in American history: An encyclopedia*, ABC-CLIO, ISBN 978-1-57607-812-9

Knight, P. (2008). Outrageous conspiracy theories: Popular and official responses to 9/11 in Germany and the United States. *New German Critique, 35,* 165–193. https://doi.org/10.1215/0094033X-2007-024

Knoblauch, M. (2016, December 30). Conspiracy theorists think an injured NBA player is another victim of Pizzagate. *Mashable*. https://mashable.com/article/bogut-pizzagate-nba-injury-conspiracy

Knock, T. J. (2019). *To end all wars, new edition: Woodrow Wilson and the quest for a new world order*. Princeton University Press. ISBN 978-0-691-19192-8.

Knoop, D., & Jones, G. P. (1947). *The genesis of freemasonry: An account of the rise and development of freemasonry in its operative, accepted and early speculative phases*. Manchester University Press.

Knowler, G. (2015, April 15). Cathay slaps blanket ban on bulk lithium battery shipments. *The Journal of Commerce*. https://www.joc.com/air-cargo/cathay-slaps-blanket-ban-bulk-lithium-battery-shipments_20150415.htm

Koebler, J. (2018, February 22). Where the "crisis actor" conspiracy theory comes from. *Vice Media.* https://www.vice.com/en/article/pammy8/what-is-a-crisis-actor-conspiracy-theory-explanation-parkland-shooting-sandy-hook.

Kranish, M., & Stern, D. (2019, July 22). As vice president, Biden said Ukraine should increase gas production. Then his son got a job with a Ukrainian gas company. *The Washington Post.* https://www.washingtonpost.com/politics/as-vice-president-biden-said-ukraine-should-increase-gas-production-then-his-son-got-a-job-with-a-ukrainian-gas-company/2019/07/21/f599f42c-86dd-11e9-98c1-e945ae5db8fb_story.html

Kroth, J. (2013). *Coup d'etat: The assassination of President John F. Kennedy.* Genotype. ASIN B00EXTGDS2.

Kucukgocmen, A., & Solaker, G. (2018, November 26). Soros foundation to close in Turkey after attack by Erdogan. *Reuters.* https://www.reuters.com/article/us-turkey-security-soros-idUSKCN1NV1K

LaCapria, K. (2016, November 21). Is Comet Ping Pong Pizzeria home to a child abuse ring led by Hillary Clinton?. *Snopes.* https://www.snopes.com/fact-check/pizzagate-conspiracy/

Lackner, J. M., Brasel, A. M., Quigley, B. M., Keefer, L., Krasner, S. S., Powell, C., et al. (2010). The ties that bind: Perceived social support, stress, and IBS in severely affected patients. *Neurogastroenterology and Motility, 22,* 893–900. https://doi.org/10.1111/j.1365-2982.2010.01516.x

Lajka, A. (2020, March 30). Drop in cellphone users in China wrongly attributed to coronavirus deaths. Associated Press. https://apnews.com/article/archive-fact-checking-8717250566

Lamb, D. G., Porges, E. C., Lewis, G. F., & Williamson, J. B. (2017). Non-invasive vagal nerve stimulation effects on hyperarousal and autonomic state in patients with posttraumatic stress disorder and history of mild traumatic brain injury: Preliminary evidence. *Frontiers of Medicine, 4,* 124. https://doi:10.3389/fmed.2017.00124

Landry, A. P., Ihm, E., Kwit, S., & Schooler, J. W. (2021). Meta-dehumanization erodes democratic norms during the 2020 presidential election. *Analyses of Social Issues and Public Policy, 21,* 51–63. https://doi.org/10.1111/asap.12253

Lao, R. C. (1978). Levenson's Internal External Control Scale. *Journal of Cross-Cultural Psychology, 9,* 113–124. https://doi.org/10.1177/002202217891009

Lazarus, R. S., & Folkman, S. (1984). *Stress, appraisal, and coping.* New York: Springer.

le Forestier, R. (1914). *Les Illuminés de Bavière et la franc-maçonnerie allemande,* Paris. pp. 453, 468–469, 507–508, 614–615.

Lee, J., Joo, E., & Choi, K. (2013). Perceived stress and self-esteem mediate the effects of work-related stress on depression. *Stress and Health, 29,* 75–81. https://doi.org/10.1002/smi.2428

Leibovitz, T., Shamblaw, A. L., Rumas, R., & Best, M. W. (2021). Covid-19 conspiracy beliefs: Relations with anxiety, quality of life, and schemas. *Personality and Individual Differences, 175,* 110704. https://doi.org/10.1016/j.paid.2021.110704

Levenson, H. (1972). Distinction within the concept of internal-external control: Development of a new scale. *Proceedings of the Annual Convention of the American Psychological Association, 7,* 261–262.

Levin, B. (2018, October 31). Trump: "A lot of people say" George Soros is funding the migrant caravan. *Vanity Fair.* https://www.vanityfair.com/news/2018/10/donald -trump-george-soros-caravan

Lewis, D. (2016, May 4). A brief history of Lee Harvey Oswald's connection to Cuba. *Smithsonian.* https://www.smithsonianmag.com/smart-news/a-brief-history-of-lee -harvey-oswalds-connection-to-cuba-180958987/

Lewis, S. (2020, November 7). No, these viral videos do not actually show election fraud. *CBS News.* https://www.cbsnews.com/news/viral-videos-do-not-show -election-fraud-evidence-donald-trump-joe-biden/

Liebowitz, J. (2021). *The business of pandemics: The COVID 19 story.* CRC Press, Taylor & Francis Group.

Lo, S., Li, S. S., & Wu, T. (2021). Exploring psychological factors for COVID-19 vaccination intention in Taiwan. *Vaccines* (Basel), 9(7), 764. https://doi.org/10 .3390/vaccines9070764

MacAskill, E. (2003, September 6). Meacher sparks fury over claims on September 11 and Iraq war Politics. *The Guardian.* https://www.theguardian.com/politics /2003/sep/06/uk.iraq

MacLeod, C., Winter, M. & Gray, A. (2014, March 8). Beijing-bound flight from

Madamidola, B. (2018, August 9). Turkey boycotts Eurovision song contest over LGBT performers. Reuters. https://www.reuters.com/article/turkey-lgbt-music -idUSL5N1V06QB

Madhani, A. (2020, June 27). What to wear: Feds' mixed messages on masks sow confusion. Associated Press. https://abcnews.go.com/Health/wireStory/wear-feds -mixed-messages-masks-sow-confusion-71491268

Mahmood, B. (2020, May 22). One fifth of English people in study blame Jews or Muslims for Covid-19. *Newsweek.* https://www.newsweek.com/Covid-19 -conspiracy-theories-england-1505899

Makow, H. (2022, January 10). The aim of freemasonry is the triumph of communism. Henrymakow.com. https://www.henrymakow.com/000280.html

Maksudyan, N. (2019) "This is a man's world?": On fathers and architects. *Journal of Genocide Research, 21,* 540–544. https://doi.org/10.1080/14623528.2019.1613816

Malaysia missing. *USA Today.* https://www.usatoday.com/story/news/world/2014/03 /07/malaysia-airlines-beijing-flight-missing/6187779

Malouse, C. (2013, November 18). Kennedy assassination: Why New Orleans is conspiracy prone. *My New Orleans.* https://www.myneworleans.com/kennedy -assassination-why-new-orleans-is-conspiracy-prone/

Mangan, D., & Breuninger, K. (2019, August 27). Jeffrey Epstein's lawyers highly "skeptical" of suicide ruling, say he wasn't "despairing, despondent" before death. CNBC. https://www.cnbc.com/2019/08/27/jeffrey-epsteins-lawyers-skeptical-of -suicide-ruling.html

Manjarres, J. (2021, May 27). Massive numbers of dead people voted in the 2020 Presidential presidential election. *The Floridian.* https://floridianpress.com/2021 /05/massive-numbers-of-dead-people-voted-in-the-2020-presidential-election/

Margolin, J. (2020, March 23). White supremacists encouraging their members to spread coronavirus to cops, Jews, FBI says. *ABC News.* https://abcnews.go .com/US/white- supremacists-encouraging-members-spread-coronavirus-cops-jews/story?id=69737522

Maricopa County Elections Department. [@MaricopaVote]. (November 5, 2020).

Marques, M. D., Ling, M., Williams, M. N., Kerr, J. R., & McLennan, J. (2022). Australasian public awareness and belief in conspiracy theories: Motivational correlates. *Political Psychology, 43,* 177–198. https://doi.org/10.1111/pops.12746

Marrian, N. (2014, April 4). Truth is Nkandla probe was long time in the making. *Business Day.* http://www.publicworks.gov.za/PDFs/NewsPapers/2014/2014 -04-04/Business_Day_page8_4April2014.pdf

Marrs, J. (2013). *Our occulted history.* William Morrow. ISBN 978-0–06–213032–7.

Mashuri, A., & Zaduqisti, E. (2015). The effect of intergroup threat and social identity salience on the belief in conspiracy theories over terrorism in Indonesia: Collective angst as a mediator. *International Journal of Psychological Research, 8,* 24–35. https://doi.org/10.21500/20112084.642

Matthews, K. A., Hall, M. H., Cousins, J., & Lee, L. (2016). Getting a good night's sleep in adolescence: Do strategies for coping with stress matter? *Behavioral Sleep Medicine, 14,* 367–377. https://doi.org/10.1080/15402002.2015.1007994

Mayor of Ankara has linked the earthquake with a conspiracy against Turkey. (2017, June 14). https://intmassmedia.com/2017/06/14/ the-mayor-of-ankara-has-linked-the-earthquake-with-a-conspiracy-against-turkey/

McCarson, M. (2012, December 14). Newtown Connecticut elementary shooting is a staged false flag against gun owners and preppers. *The Last Defense Blog.* https://tld2012blog.wordpress.com/2012/12/17/newtown-connecticut-elementary -shooting-is-a/

McCarthy, M., Murphy, K., Sargeant, E., & Williamson, H. (2021). Examining the relationship between conspiracy theories and COVID-19 vaccine hesitancy: A mediating role for perceived health threats, trust, and anomie? *Analyses of Social Issues and Public Policy,* https://doi.org/10.1111/asap.12291

McCoy, R. (2015). Future operations of HAARP with the UAF's UAF's geophysical institute. *AGU Fall Meeting Abstracts. American Geophysical Union Fall Meeting.* Bibcode:2015AGUFMAE22A..07M.

McEnany, K. [@kayleighmcenany]. (Nov 6, 2020).

McKie, R. (2019, Nov 9). Climategate 10 years on: what lessons have we learned? *The Guardian.* https://www.theguardian.com/theobserver/2019/nov/09/climategate -10-years-on-what-lessons-have-we-learned.

McNamara, A. (2020, November 1). Trump spreads baseless claim about Dominion Voting Systems after losing election. *CBS News.* https://www.cbsnews.com/news/ trump-dominion-voting-systems-false-accusation/

Medina, S., & Spriester, M. (2018, February 6). 700 rounds in 11 minutes: Sutherland Springs survivor says he's amazed he's alive. *KSAT.* https://www.ksat.com/

news/2018/02/06/700-rounds-in-11-minutes-sutherland-springs-survivor-says-hes
-amazed-hes-alive

Merton, R. (1968). *Social theory and social structure*. 1968 enl. ed. New York: Free Press.

Meyssan, T. (2002). *9/11: The big lie*. Gardners Books. Eastbourne, UK. ISBN-10: 2912362733.

MH17: The Netherlands and Australia hold Russia responsible. (2018, May 25). *Government of the Netherlands*. https://www.government.nl/latest/news/2018 /05/25/mh17-the-netherlands-and-australia-hold-russia-responsible

MH370 search: Mozambique debris "almost certainly" from missing plane. (2016, March 24). *BBC News*. https://www.bbc.com/news/world-asia-35888405

MH370—Definition of Underwater Search Areas. (2014, June 26). *Australian Transport Safety Bureau*. https://www.atsb.gov.au/media/news items/2015/mh370 -definition of underwater search areas/

Mikkelson, D. (2011, August 27). Fact Checkcheck: Is Barack Obama's birth certificate fake? *Snopes*. https://www.snopes.com/fact-check/birth-certificate/

Misiak, B., Samochowiec, J., Bhui, K., Schouler-Ocak, M., Demunter, H., Kuey, L., Raballo, A., Gorwood, P., Frydecka, D., & Dom, G. (2019). A systematic review on the relationship between mental health, radicalization and mass violence. *European Psychiatry, 56*, 51–59. https://doi.org/10.1016/j.eurpsy.2018.11.005

Mitchell, J. M., Bogenschutz, M., Lilienstein, A., Harrison, C., Kleiman, S., Parker-Guilbert, K. et al. (2021). MDMA-assisted therapy for severe PTSD: A randomized, double-blind, placebo-controlled phase 3 study. *Nature Medicine, 27*, 1025–2033. https://doi.org/10.1038/d41591-021-01336-3

Moghadam, A. (2008). *The globalization of martyrdom: Al Qaeda, Salafi Jihadjihad, and the diffusion of suicide attacks*. Johns Hopkins University Press. p. 48. ISBN 978-0-8018-9055-0.

Moon, D. (2013). Powerful emotions: Symbolic power and the (productive and punitive) force of collective feeling. *Theory and Society, 42*, 261–294. https://doi.org /10.1007/s11186-013-9190-3

Morkved, N., Hartmann, K., Aarsheim, L. M., Holen, D., Milde, A. M., Bomyea, J., et al. (2014). A comparison of narrative exposure therapy and prolonged exposure therapy for PTSD. *Clinical Psychology Review, 34*, 453–467. https://doi.org/10 .1016/j.cpr.2014.06.005

Morris, B., & Ze'"evi, D. (2019). *The thirty-year genocide: Turkey's Destruction destruction of Its its Christian Minoritiesminorities, 1894–1924*. Harvard University Press.

Morris, C. (2001, December 23). 9/11: bin Laden '"confession' confession" video mistranslated and manipulated by the CIA. *Empire Strikes Black*. http: //empirestrikesblack.com/2011/05/911-bin-laden-confession-video-mistranslated -and-manipulated-by-the-cia/

Morton, J. (2016, August 10). WikiLeaks offers $20,000 reward for help finding Omaha native Seth Rich's killer. *Omaha World-Herald*. https://omaha.com/news /crime/wikileaks-offers-20-000-reward-for-help-finding-omaha-native-seth-richs -killer/article_cfb287bc-5e98-11e6-ae0c-8b471b8cbfbb.html

Moseley, R. L., Turner-Cobb, J. M., Spahr, C. M., Shields, G. S., & Slavich, G. M. (2021). Lifetime and perceived stress, social support, loneliness, and health in autistic adults. *Health Psychology, 40*, 556–568. https://doi.org/10.1037/hea0001108

Moynihan, M. (2012, December 27). Newtown conspiracy theories: Obama, Iran, and other culprits. *The Daily Beast.* https://www.thedailybeast.com/newtown-conspiracy-theories-obama-iran-and-other-culprits

Mullen, J. (2014, September 9). Report: MH17 hit by burst of "high-energy objects" from outside. CNN. https://www.cnn.com/2014/09/09/world/europe/netherlands-ukraine-mh17-report/index.html

Murdoch, M., Spoont, M. R., Sayer, N. A., Kehle-Forbes, S. M., & Noorbaloochi, S. (2021). Reversals in initially denied department of veterans affairs' PTSD disability claims after 17 years: A cohort study of gender differences. *BMC Women's Health, 21*:, 70. https://doi.org/10.1186/s12905-021-01214-7

Mus, M., Bor, A., & Bang Petersen, M. (2022). Do conspiracy theories efficiently signal coalition membership? an An experimental test using the "who said what?" design. *PloS One, 17*, e0265211–e0265211. https://doi.org/10.1371/journal.pone.0265211

Najavits, L. M. (2002). *Seeking Safetysafety: A treatment manual for PTSD and substance abuse.* New York, NY: Guilford Press.

Naqi, K. (2015, February 18). Patriot's locker room attendant tried to put unapproved ball into AFC final. *ABC News* https://abcnews.go.com/Sports/patriots-locker-room-attendant-put-unapproved-ball-afc/story?id=29040309

National Livestock Identification System. (2013, August 20, 2013). *Meat & Livestock Australia Limited.* https://www.nlis.com.au/

Natoli, E. E., & Marques, M. D. (2021) The antidepressant hoax: Conspiracy theories decrease health-seeking intentions. *British Journal of Social Psychology, 60*, 902–923. https://doi.org/10.1111/bjso.12426

Neiwert, D. (2009, March 17). FEMA concentration camps? The militia good times are rollin' again. *Crooks and Liars.* https://crooksandliars.com/david-neiwert/fema-concentration-camps-militia-goo

Nelson, L. (2011, December 20). Coming full circle: FEMA camp theory gains traction on far left. *Southern Poverty Law Center.* https://www.splcenter.org/hatewatch/2011/12/20/coming-full-circle-fema-camp-theory-gains-traction-far-left

New conspiracy theories embroil the New England Patriots. (2018, January 31). *The Big Think.* https://bigthink.com/politics-current-affairs/new-conspiracy-theories-embroil-the-new-england-patriots/

Newheiser, A., Farias, M., & Tausch, N. (2011). The functional nature of conspiracy beliefs: Examining the underpinnings of belief in the Da Vinci Code conspiracy. *Personality and Individual Differences, 51*, 1007–1011. https://doi.org/10.1016/j.paid.2011.08.011

Nicas, J. (2020, November 12). No, Dominion voting machines did not delete Trump votes. *The New York Times.* https://www.nytimes.com/2020/11/11/technology/no-dominion-voting-machines-did-not-delete-trump-votes.html

Nigerian president apologizes for plagiarizing Obama in speech. (2016, September 17). *The Guardian*. https://www.theguardian.com/world/2016/sep/17/nigerian -president-apologizes-for-plagiarizing-obama-in-speech

Norris, C. M., & Mitchell, F. D. (2014). Exploring the stress-support-distress process among Black women. *Journal of Black Studies, 45*, 3–18. https://doi.org/10.1177 /0021934713517898

O'Brien, M. (2018, August 8). Turkey is fighting an "economic war"—against reality." *The Washington Post*. https://www.washingtonpost.com/business/2018/08 /08/turkeys-erdogan-says-hes-fighting-an-economic-war-hes-right-its-war-against -reality/

Olding, R. (2020, October 17). Steve Bannon boasted on Dutch TV weeks ago that he had Hunter Biden's hard drive. *The Daily Beast*. https://www.thedailybeast.com /steve-bannon-boasted-on-dutch-tv-weeks-ago-that-he-had-hunter-bidens hard -drive

Osama tape appears fake, experts conclude. (2006, June 1). *Looking Glass News*. http: //www.lookingglassnews.org/viewstory.php?storyid=6233

Osborne, H. (2020, July 30). U.S. moon landing was a hoax, half of Russians believe. *Newsweek*. https://www.newsweek.com/moon-landing-hoax-russia-poll-1521595

Palamara, V. (1997). *The third alternative—Survivor's guilt: The Secret Service and the JFK murder*. Southlake: JFK Lancer Productions & Publications. ISBN 0–9656582–4–4.

Palma, B. (2017, May 16). Fact check: Did DNC staffer Seth Rich send "thousands of Ee-mails" to WikiLeaks before he was murdered? *Snopes*. https://www.snopes .com/fact-check/seth-rich-dnc-wikileaks-murder/

Panagioti, M., Gooding, P. A., Taylor, P. J., & Tarrier, N. (2014). Perceived social support buffers the impact of PTSD symptoms on suicidal behavior: Implications into suicide resilience research. *Comprehensive Psychiatry, 55*, 104–112. https://doi.org /10.1016/j.comppsych.2013.06.004

Paracha, N. F. (2013, October 10). Malala: The Real real Story story (with Evidenceevidence). *Dawn*. https://www.dawn.com/news/1048776

Pasek, J, Stark, T, Krosnick, J., & Tompson, T.(2015). What motivates a conspiracy theory? Dirther beliefs, partisanship, liberal-conservative ideology, and anti-Black attitudes. *Electoral Studies, 40*, 482–489. https://doi.10.1016/j.electstud.2014.09 .009. ISSN 0261-3794

Patterson, D. (2020, September 2). Top U.S. cybersecurity expert on mail-in voting: "If you've got paper, you've got receipts." *CBS News*. https://www.cbsnews.com/ news/mail-in-voting-cybersecurity-hackers-2020-elections/

Payne, C., Spunt, D., Yingst, T., Griffin, J., & Cavuto, N. (2022). Gas prices rising; pentagon updates ukraine crisis; interview with Bank of America CEO Brian Moynihan; Russian invasion of Ukraine imminent? CQ Roll Call.

Payne, K. (2017). *The broken ladder: How inequality affects the way we think, live, and die*. Viking Press.

Peck, J. (2016, November 28). What the hell is #Pizzagate?" *Death and Taxes*. http:// www.deathandtaxesmag.com/311037/pizzagate-podesta-pedophiles/

Pengelly, M. (2020, December 21). Conspiracy-theorist lawyer Sidney Powell spotted again at White House. *The Guardian.* https://www.theguardian.com/us-news/2020 /dec/21/sidney-powell-conspiracy-theorist-white-house

Phillips, D. (2010, July 1). Conspiracy theories behind BP oil spill in gulf-From Dick Cheney to UFOs. *CBS News.* https://www.cbsnews.com/news/conspiracy-theories -behind-bp-oil-spill-in-gulf-from-dick-cheney-to-ufos/

Piller, C. (2020, July 16). Data secrecy is crippling attempts to slow COVID-19's spread in U.S., epidemiologists warn. *Science Magazine.* https://www.science .org/content/article/us-epidemiologists-say-data-secrecy-Covid-19-cases-cripples -intervention-strategies

Pitcavage, M. (2001). Camouflage and conspiracy. The militia movement from ruby ridge to Y2K. *American Behavioral Scientist, 44,* 957–981. https://doi.org/10.1177 /00027640121956610

Plait, P. (2002). *Bad Astronomyastronomy: Misconceptions and misuses revealed, from astrology to the moon landing "hoax."* New York: John Wiley & Sons. ISBN 0–471–40976–6.

Poladian, C. (2013, July 22). CIA exploring geoengineering, ways to control weather, to reverse global warming: Report. *International Business Times.* https://www .ibtimes.com/cia-exploring-geoengineering-ways-control-weather-reverse-globing -warming-report-1356093

Pomcranz, J. L., & Schwid, A.R. (2021). Governmental actions to address COVID-19 misinformation. *Journal of Public Health Policy.* 42, 201–210. https://doi.org/10 .1057/s41271-020-00270-x

Poon, K., Chen, Z., & Wong, W. (2020). Beliefs in conspiracy theories following ostracism. *Personality and Social Psychology Bulletin, 46,* 1234–1246. https://doi .org/10.1177/0146167219898944

Poteshman, A. (2006). Unusual option market activity and terrorist attacks of September 11, 2001. *The Journal of Business, 79,* 703.- https://doi:10.1086 /503645. S2CID 153626942

Pratt, R. (2003). Theorizing conspiracy. *Theory and Society, 32,* 255–271. https://doi .org/10.1023/A:1023996501425

Preacher, K. J., & Hayes, A. F. (2004). SPSS and SAS procedures for estimating indirect effects in simple mediation models. *Behavior Research Methods, Instruments, and Computers, 36,* 717–731. https://doi.org/10.3758/BF03206553

Prichard, E. C., & Christman, S. D. (2020). Authoritarianism, conspiracy beliefs, gender and COVID-19: Links between individual differences and concern about COVID-19, mask wearing behaviors, and the tendency to blame China for the virus. *Frontiers in Psychology, 11,* 597671–597671. https://doi.org/10.3389/fpsyg .2020.597671

Profiting from disaster? (2001, September 19). *CBS News.* https://www.cbsnews.com /news/profiting-from-disaster/

Putterman, S. (2020, February 10). Facebook post Says says Paul Walker was set to come forward to expose "Clinton Foundation crimes against children in Haiti" before he was killed. *Politifact.* https://www.politifact.com/factchecks/2020/feb/10 /facebook-posts/no-evidence-support-paul-walker-clinton-conspiracy/

Putz, C. (2021, April 15). Biden Announces announces Plan plan for US Exit exit from Afghan Warwar, Urges urges Attention attention to Future future Challengeschallenges. *The Diplomat.* https://thediplomat.com/2021/04/biden-announces-plan-for-us-exit-from-afghan-war-urges-attention-to-future-challenges/

QAnon: A Glossaryglossary. (2021, January 21). Anti-Defamation League. https://www.adl.org/blog/qanon-a-glossary

Quinn, M. (2020a, August 26). Trump targets ballot drop boxes in effort to discredit vote-by-mail. *CBS News.* https://www.cbsnews.com/news/trump-mail-in-voting-ballot-drop-boxes/

Quinn, M. (2020b, November 6). Fact-checking Trump's claims on poll watchers. *CBS News.* https://www.cbsnews.com/news/fact-check-trumps-claims-poll-watchers/

Rabkin, F. (2015, September 15). DA joins EFF in Nkandla court case. *Business Day.* http://www.bdlive.co.za/national/politics/2015/09/15/da-joins-eff-in-nkandla-court-case

Radnitz, S., & Underwood, P. (2017). Is belief in conspiracy theories pathological? A survey experiment on the cognitive roots of extreme suspicion. *British Journal of Political Science, 47,* 113–129. https://doi.org/10.1017/S0007123414000556

Rauhala E., Paquette D., & George S (May 15, 2020). Polio was almost eradicated. Then came the coronavirus. Then came a threat from President Trump. *The Washington Post.* https://www.washingtonpost.com/world/polio-was-almost-eradicated-then-came-the-coronavirus-then-came-a-threat-from-president-trump/2020/05/15/ed9d26fe-831c-11ea-81a3-9690c9881111_story.html

Reidy, P. (2014, July 22). MH17: five of the most bizarre conspiracy theories. *The Guardian.* https://www.theguardian.com/commentisfree/2014/jul/22/mh17-five-bizarre-conspiracy-theories-zionist-plots-illuminati-russian-tv

Renegade bird accused of being an Israeli spy cleared after careful examination in Turkey. (2013, July 25). *Hürriyet Daily News.* July 25, 2013. https://www.hurriyetdailynews.com/renegade-bird-accused-of-being-an-israeli-spy-cleared-after-careful-examination-in-turkey-51440

Reports that Putin flew similar route as MH17, presidential airport says "hasn't overflown Ukraine for long time." (2014, July 17) *RT.* https://www.rt.com/news/173672-malaysia-plane-crash-putin/

Resume of Thuli Madonsela. *ANC.* https://web.archive.org/web/20140903095847/http://www.anc.org.za/caucus/show.php?ID=2001

Rizzo, S. (2018, October 5). No, George Soros isn't paying Kavanaugh protesters. *The Washington Post.* https://www.washingtonpost.com/politics/2018/10/05/no-george-soros-isnt-paying-kavanaugh-protesters/

Robertson, P. (1991). *The new world order.* W Pub Group.

Rodrigo Duterte: "I'm not joking——clean masks with petrol." (2020, July 31). *BBC News.* https://www.bbc.com/news/world-asia-53605108

Romer, D., & Jamieson, K. H. (2020). Conspiracy theories as barriers to controlling the spread of COVID-19 in the U.S. *Social Science Medicine, 263,* 113356. https://doi.org/10.1016/j.socscimed.2020.11356

Rosenthal, J. (2010, September 21). German protestors marked 9/11 by denouncing "inside job," "Reichstag Fire." *Washington Examiner*. https://www .washingtonexaminer.com/weekly-standard/german-protestors-marked-9-11-by -denouncing-inside-job-reichstag-fire

Routledge, C., Abeyta, A. A., & Roylance, C. (2017). We are not alone: The meaning motive, religiosity, and belief in extra-terrestrial intelligence. *Motivation and Emotion, 41,* 135–146. https://doi.org/10.1007/s11031-017-9605-y

Safety worries lead U.S. airline to ban battery shipments. (2015, March 3). *BBC News.* https://www.bbc.com/news/technology-31709198

Sapountzis, A., & Condor, S. (2013). Conspiracy accounts as intergroup theories: Challenging dominant understandings of social power and political legitimacy. *Political Psychology, 34,* 731–752. https://doi.org/10.1111/pops.12015

Saul, S., & Hakim, D. (2020, November 4). As counting begins, a flood of mail ballots complicates vote tallies. *The New York Times* https://www.nytimes.com/2020 /11/03/us/elections/mail-ballot-counting-vote.html

Schadewald, R. (July 1980). The flat-out truth: Earth orbits? Moon landings? A fraud! says this prophet. *Science Digest*. New York: Hearst Magazines. Retrieved April 15, 2022.

Schaff, P., & Wace, H. (1890). *Sulpitius Severus*. Christian Classics Ethereal Library. https://ccel.org/ccel/schaff/npnf211/npnf211.ii.i.html

Schulberg, J. (2020, November 4). Trump allies are pushing #SharpieGate conspiracy theory to claim election theft. *Huffpost*. https://www.huffpost.com/entry/trump -allies-sharpiegate-conspiracy-theory_n_5fa312c9c5b69c36d951dc9e

Segir Panama-skjölin runnin undan rifjum Soros. (2016, July 27). *RÚV*. https://www .ruv.is/frett/segir-panama-skjolin-runnin-undan-rifjum-soros

Selk, A., & Grant, M. (2017, November 6). A fake shooter and "false flag" rumors at the hospital——how dark online hoaxes came to Texas. *The Washington Post*. https://www.washingtonpost.com/news/the-intersect/wp/2017/11/06/a-fake -shooter-and-false-flag-rumors-at-the-hospital-how-dark-online-hoaxes-came-to -texas/

Senz, K. (2007, June 19). Browns say they will either walk free, or die. *New Hampshire Union Leader* https://www.unionleader.com/article.aspx?headline=Bro wns+say+they+will+either+walk+free%2c+or+die&articleId=a02db0e8-8042 -474e-8a82-1fb5dc2f6306

Shachtman, N. (2009, July 20). Strange new Air Force facility energizes ionosphere, fans conspiracy flames. *Wired Magazine*. https://www.wired.com/2009/07/mf -haarp/

Shane, S., Vogel, K., & Kingsley, P. (2018, October 31). How vilification of George Soros moved from the fringes to the mainstream. *The New York Times*. https://www .nytimes.com/2018/10/31/us/politics/george-soros-bombs-trump.html

Shenon, P. (2011, August 11). September 11th anniversary: an An explosive new 9/11 charge. *The Daily Beast*. https://www.thedailybeast.com/september-11th -anniversary-richard-clarkes-explosive-cia-cover-up-charge

Sherwell, P. (2020, December 6). Leak exposes how Beijing ordered under-reporting of Wuhan coronavirus cases. *The Times*. https://www.thetimes.co.uk/article/

leak-exposes-how-beijing-ordered-under-reporting-of-wuhan-coronavirus-cases
-q8rc2hhkd

Sheth, S. (2022, March 19). Marie Yovanovitch says Rudy Giuliani was Trump's "personal dirt-digger" and corrupt Ukrainians used him to spread "lies and half-truths" in the US. *Business Insider*. https://www.businessinsider.nl/marie-yovanovitch-says-rudy-giuliani-was-trumps-personal-dirt-digger-and-corrupt-ukrainians-used-him-to-spread-lies-and-half-truths-in-the-us/

Shishehgar, S., Mahmoodi, A., Dolatian, M., Mahmoodi, Z., Bakhtiary, M., & Alavi Majd, H. (2013). The relationship of social support and quality of life with the level of stress in pregnant women using the PATH model. *Iranian Red Crescent Medical Journal, 15*, 560–565. https://doi.org/10.5812/ircmj.12174

Simione, L., Vagni, M., Gnagnarella, C., Bersani, G., & Pajardi, D. (2021). Mistrust and beliefs in conspiracy theories differently mediate the effects of psychological factors on propensity for COVID-19 vaccine. *Frontiers in Psychology, 12*, 683684–683684. https://doi.org/10.3389/fpsyg.2021.683684

Simons, P. (2013, September 13). Weather eye: contrail conspiracy. *The Times*. https://www.thetimes.co.uk/article/weather-eye-contrail-conspiracy-sx8twmq55b6

Singman, B. (2018, May 14). First lady Melania Trump in hospital, underwent "'successful" kidney procedure. *Fox News*. https://www.foxnews.com/politics/first-lady-melania-trump-in-hospital-underwent-successful-kidney-procedure

Sipalan, J. (2019, June 21). Russians made a "'scapegoat" after MH17 report released, says Malaysia PM. *The Sydney Morning Herald*. https://www.smh.com.au/world/europe/putin-claims-no-proof-russians-downed-mh17-20190621-p51ztv.html

Smith-Spark, L., & Masters, J. (2018, May 24). Missile that downed MH17 "owned by Russian brigade." CNN. https://www.cnn.com/2018/05/24/europe/mh17-plane-netherlands-russia-intl/index.html

Smith, C., Hancock, H., Blake-Mortimer, J., & Eckert, K. (2007). A randomized comparative trial of yoga and relaxation to reduce stress and anxiety. *Complementary Therapies in Medicine, 15*, 77–83. https://doi.org/10.1016/j.ctim.2006.05.001

Smith, M. (2015, July 15). In Bastrop, Jade Helm begins with a whimper. *Texas Tribune*. https://www.texastribune.org/2015/07/15/bastrop-jade-helm-begins/.

Smith, O. (2013, September 24). Chemtrails'' and other aviation conspiracy theories. *The Telegraph*. https://www.telegraph.co.uk/travel/news/chemtrails-contrails-and-other-aviation-conspiracy-theories/

Solman, P., Schifrin, N., Sy, S., Desjardins, L., & Woodruff, J. (2021). *PBS NewsHour for June 8, 2021*. CQ Roll Call.

Solnit, R. (2021, January 6). The violence at the Capitol was an attempted coup. Call it that. *The Guardian*. https://www.theguardian.com/commentisfree/2021/jan/06/trump-mob-storm-capitol-washington-coup-attempt

Sozeri, E. (2016, November 23). How the alt-right's PizzaGate conspiracy hid real scandal in Turkey. *The Daily Dot*. https://www.dailydot.com/debug/pizzagate-alt-right-turkey-trolls-child-abuse/

Spencer, S.H. (2020, September 1). CDC did not "admit only 6%" of recorded deaths from COVID-19. *FactCheck.org*. https://www.factcheck.org/2020/09/cdc-did-not-admit-only-6-of-recorded-deaths-from-covid-19/

Spollen, M. (2017, September 2). Bizarre rumors and conspiracy theories that claim Linkin Park lead singer Chester Bennington was murdered. *Your Tango*. https://www.yahoo.com/lifestyle/bizarre-rumors-conspiracy-theories-claim-045340117.html

Šrol, J., Ballová Mikušková, E., & Čavojová, V. (2021). When we are worried, what are we thinking? Anxiety, lack of control, and conspiracy beliefs amidst the COVID-19 pandemic. *Applied Cognitive Psychology, 35*, 720–729. https://doi.org/10.1002/acp.3798

Stein, J. (2016, August 20). Seth Rich: Inside the killing of the DNC staffer. *Newsweek*. https://www.newsweek.com/2016/09/16/seth-rich-murder-dnc-hack-julian-assange-hillary-clinton-donald-trump-492084.html

Stephan, W. G., Craig, T., & Gregory, W. L. (1999). Beliefs in conspiracies. *Political Psychology, 20*, 637–47. https://doi.org/10.1111/0162-895X.00160

Sternisko, A., Cichocka, A., Cislak, A., & Van Bavel, J. J. (2021). National narcissism predicts the belief in and the dissemination of conspiracy theories during the COVID-19 pandemic: Evidence from 56 countries. *Personality and Social Psychology Bulletin*, https://doi.org/10.1177/01461672211054947

Stroope, S., Kroeger, R. A., Williams, C. E., & Baker, J. O. (2021). Sociodemographic correlates of vaccine hesitancy in the United States and the mediating role of beliefs about governmental conspiracies. *Social Science Quarterly, 102*, 2472–81. https://doi.org/10.1111/ssqu.13081

Suny, R. (2015). *They can live in the desert but nowhere else: A history of the Armenian Genocidegenocide*. Princeton University Press. ISBN 978-1-4008-6558-1.

Sushant Singh Rajput's fault is that he believed those who called him "worthless," says Kangana Ranaut in passionate video. (2020, June 15). *Hindustan Times*. https://www.hindustantimes.com/bollywood/sushant-singh-rajput-s-fault-is-that-he-believed-those-who-called-him-worthless-says-kangana-ranaut-in-passionate-video/story-PU8XYbq6wloAJCkoACY5tM.html

Swaine, J. (2011, April 27). Birther row began with Hillary Clinton supporters. *The Telegraph*. https://www.telegraph.co.uk/news/worldnews/barackobama/8478044/Birther-row-began-with-Hillary-Clinton-supporters.html

Swami, V. (2012). Social psychological origins of conspiracy theories: The case of the Jewish conspiracy theory in Malaysia. *Frontiers in Psychology, 3:*, 280. https://doi.org/fpsyg.2012.00280

Swami, V., Furnham, A., Smyth, N., Weis, L., Lay, A., & Clow, A. (2016). Putting the stress on conspiracy theories: Examining associations between psychological stress, anxiety, and belief in conspiracy theories. *Personality and Individual Differences, 99*, 72–76. https://doi.org/10.1016/j.paid.2016.04.084

Swanson, G. (2003). Dennis Fisin (ed.). *Ground Zero, A collection of personal accounts*. TRAC Team. http://www.digitalstylecreations.com/Download/BlackBoxStory.html

Sydne, J. P. (2014, June 30). MH370 investigators find evidence of a mysterious power outage during the early part of its flight. *The Telegraph*. https://www.businessinsider.com/mh370-investigators-find-evidence-of-a-mysterious-power-outage-during-the-early-part-of-its-flight-2014-6

Sykes, L. (2009, May 17). *Angels & Demons* causing serious controversy. *KFSN-TV/ABC News.* https://abc30.com/archive/6817493/

Tada, A. (2017). The associations among psychological distress, coping style, and health habits in Japanese nursing students: A cross-sectional study. *International Journal of Environmental Research and Public Health, 14:,*1434. https://doi.org /10.3390/ijerph14111434

Tajfel, H. (1974). Social identity and intergroup behavior. *Social Science Information, 13,* 65–93. https://doi.org/10.1177/053901847401300204

Tarbert, K. (2020, November 3) Fake Melania: White House insider confirms rumors. *Yahoo Lifestyle!* https://au.lifestyle.yahoo.com/fake-melania-rumors-confirmed -white-house-anthony-scaramucci-012905419.html

Taylor, A. (2015, June 8). The "Obama is a Muslim" conspiracy theory gets a Shiite twist from a former Iraqi lawmaker. *The Washington Post.* https://www .washingtonpost.com/news/worldviews/wp/2015/06/08

Taylor, J. (2020, January 31). Bat soup, dodgy cures and "diseasology"": The spread of coronavirus misinformation. *The Guardian.* https://www.theguardian.com/world /2020/jan/31/bat-soup-dodgy-cures-and-diseasology-the-spread-of-coronavirus -bunkum

Teh, C. (2021, August 25). A Texas father stripped down to his underwear during a school-board meeting to make a point about wearing masks. MSN. https: //www.msn.com/en-us/lifestyle/lifestyle-buzz/a-texas-father-stripped-down-to-his -underwear-during-a-school-board-meeting-to-make-a-point-about-wearing-masks /ar-AANKIkn.

Texas officials: Mass shooting not motivated by religion or race. (2017, November 6). WREG-TV. https://wreg.com/news/texas-officials-mass-shooting-not-motivated -by-religion-or-race/

Texas shooting death toll includes unborn child. (2017, November 7). Associated Press. https://fox40.com/news/national-and-world-news/texas-shooting-death-toll -includes-unborn-child/

Than, K. (2009, July 20). Photos: 8 moon-landing hoax myths——busted. *National Geographic.* https://www.nationalgeographic.com/science/article/apollo-11-hoax -photos--8-moon-landing-myths-busted

The 2020 voting experience: Coronavirus, mail concerns factored into deciding how to vote. (2020, November 20). *Pew Research Center.* https://www.pewresearch.org /politics/2020/11/20/the-voting-experience-in-2020/

The Barack Obama illuminati connection. (2009, August 1). *The Best of Rush Limbaugh Featured Sites.* Retrieved April 16, 2022

Theadom, A., Cropley, M., & Humphrey, K. (2007). Exploring the role of sleep and coping in quality of life in fibromyalgia. *Journal of Psychosomatic Research, 62,* 145–151. https://doi.org/10.1016/j.jpsychores.2006.09.013

Timm, J., & Johnstone, L. (2019, August 10). Trump retweets Epstein conspiracy theory, claiming Clinton connection. *NBC News.* https://www.nbcnews.com/ politics/donald-trump/trump-retweets-epstein-conspiracy-theory-claiming-clinton -connection-n1041146

Tomasky, M. (2011, April 27). Birthers and the persistence of racial paranoia. *The Guardian.* https://www.theguardian.com/commentisfree/michaeltomasky/2011/apr/27/barack-obama-obama-administration

Tonković, M., Dumančić, F., Jelić, M., & Čorkalo Biruški, D. (2021). Who believes in COVID-19 conspiracy theories in Croatia? Prevalence and predictors of conspiracy beliefs. *Frontiers in Psychology, 12,* 643568. https://doi.org/10.3389/fpsyg.2021.643568

Tracy, J. (2012, December 24). The Sandy Hook massacre: Unanswered questions and missing information. *Memory Hole.* https://memoryholeblog.org/2012/12/24/the-sandy-hook-massacre-unanswered-questions-and-missing-information/

Trew, B. (2020, March 27). Coronavirus: Hundreds dead in Iran from drinking methanol amid fake reports it cures disease. *The Independent.* https://www.independent.co.uk/news/world/middle-east/iran-coronavirus-methanol-drink-cure-deaths-fake-a9429956.html

Trial and triumph: Stories out of Africa (2008, October 9). NPR. https://www.npr.org/2008/10/09/95550177/trial-and-triumph-stories-out-of-africa

Triomphe, C. (2020, November 6). Explaining 'stop Stop the Steal,," Trump supporters'" viral offensive to discredit the election. *CTV News.* https://www.ctvnews.ca/mobile/world/america-votes/explaining-stop-the-steal-trump-supporters-viral-offensive-to-discredit-the-election-1.5177864?clipId=89619

Turner, J. C., Brown, R. J., & Tajfel, H. (1979). Social comparison and group interest in ingroup favoritism. *European Journal of Social Psychology, 9,* 187–204. https://doi.org/10.1002/ejsp.2420090207

Twelve taken ill after consuming "coronavirus shaped" datura seeds. (2020, April 7). *The Hindu.* https://www.thehindu.com/news/national/andhra-pradesh/twelve-taken-ill-after-consuming-coronavirus-shaped-datura-seeds/article31282688.ece

Tymoshenko, V. (2017). Political and legal characteristics of extremism. *ScienceRise: Juridical Science, 2,* 21–25. https://doi.org/10.15587/2523-4153.2017.116078

Uko, N. (December 2003). *Romancing the gun: The press as promoter of military rule.* Africa World Press. ISBN 978-1-59221-189-0.

Ulrich-Lai, Y. M., Christiansen, A. M., Ostrander, M. M., Jones, A. A., Jones, K. R., Choi, D. C., & McEwen, B. S. (2010). Pleasurable behaviors reduce stress via brain reward pathways. *Proceedings of the National Academy of Sciences of the United States of America, 107,* 20529–34. https://doi.org/10.1073/pnas.1007740107

United 93: Full transcript. (2006, April 13). *The Guardian.* https://www.theguardian.com/world/2006/apr/13/usa.september11

Uscinski, J. E., & Parent, J. M. (2014). *American conspiracy theories.* Oxford University Press. https://doi.org/10.1093/acprof:oso/9780199351800.001.0001

Uscinski, J., Douglas, K., & Lewandowsky, S. (2017, Sep 27). Climate change conspiracy theories. *Oxford Research Encyclopedia of Climate* Science. doi:10.1093/acrefore/9780190228620.013.328

Vaccine holdouts are caving to mandates—then scrambling to "undo" it. (2021, November 12). *NBC News.* https://www.nbcphiladelphia.com/news/national-international/covid-vaccine-holdouts-are-caving-to-mandates-then-scrambling-to-undo-their-shots/3045786/

Valby, K. (2020, January 26). SNL Drags drags Adam Driver's Jeffrey Epstein to Hell. *Vanity Fair.* https://www.vanityfair.com/hollywood/2020/01/adam-driver-snl -jeffrey-epstein-kylo-ren

Valiente-Gomez, A., Moreno-Alcazar, A., Treen, D., Cedron, C., Colom, F., Perez, V., et al. (2017). EMDR beyond PTSD: A systematic literature review. *Frontiers in Psychology, 8.* https://doi.org/10.3389/fpsyg.2017.01668

van Dülmen, R. (1992). *The Society of Enlightenment.* Polity Press., p. 110.

van Prooijen, J. W. (2016). Why education predicts decreased belief in conspiracy theories. *Applied Cognitive Psychology, 31,* 50–58. https://doi.org/10.1002/acp .3301

van Prooijen, J. W., & Song, M. (2020;). The cultural dimension of intergroup conspiracy theories. *British Journal of Psychology, 112,* 455–473. https://doi.org/10 .1111/bjop.12471

van Zyl Smit R., Richards G., & Leone F. (July 2020). Tobacco smoking and COVID-19 infection. *The Lancet: Respiratory Medicine, 8,* 664–665. https://doi.org/10 .1016/S2213-2600(20)30239-3

Ventura, J. (2013). *They killed our president.* New York: Skyhorse Publishing., p. xii.. ISBN 1626361398.

Wan, W., & Liu, L. (2014, March 10). Vanished Malaysia Airlines flight leaves relatives with anger and phantom phone calls. *The Washington Post.* https://www .washingtonpost.com/world/vanished-malaysia-airlines-flight-leaves-relatives -with-anger-and-phantom-phone-calls/2014/03/10/fdb78642-a862-11e3-b61e -8051b8b52d06_story.html

Was the Apollo moon landing fake?. (2009, July 21). *American Patriot Friends Network* https://web.archive.org/web/20180516174114/http://www.apfn.org/apfn/ moon.htm

Watson, K.. (2020, December 8). Sidney Powell lawsuit aimed at decertifying Georgia results dismissed. *CBS News.* https://www.cbsnews.com/news/sidney -powell-kraken-election-lawsuit-dismissed-georgia/#:~:text=Attorney%20Sidney %20Powell%27s%20case%20alleging%20widespread%20voter%20fraud,to %20challenge%20the%20legitimacy%20of%20the%20presidential%20election

Welch, W., & Joyner, C. (2010, May 25). Memorial service honors 11 dead oil rig workers. *USA Today* https://usatoday30.usatoday.com/news/nation/2010 05 25 oil -spill-victims-memorial_N.htm

Were Israelis detained on Sept. 11 spies? (2002, June 21). *ABC News.* https://abcnews .go.com/2020/story?id=123885&page=1

West, K., Greenland, K., & Laar, C. (2021). Implicit racism, color blindness, and narrow definitions of discrimination: Why some white people prefer "All lives Lives matterMatter" to "Black lives matter.." *British Journal of Social Psychology, 60,* 1136–1153. https://doi.org/10.1111/bjso.12458

Whiskeyman, A., & Berger, M. (2021, February 25). Axis of disinformation: Propaganda from Iran, Russia, and China on COVID-19. *The Washington Institute for Near East Policy.* https://www.washingtoninstitute.org/policy-analysis/axis -disinformation-propaganda-iran-russia-and-china-Covid-19

Whitehouse, J. (2017, May 27). How the murder of a DNC staffer turned into a right-wing conspiracy. *Salon.* https://www.salon.com/2017/05/27/how-the-murder -of-a-dnc-staffer-turned-into-a-right-wing-conspiracy_partner/

WHO did not warn against eating cabbage during the COVID-19 pandemic. (2020, April 1). *AFP Fact Check.* https://factcheck.afp.com/who-did-not-warn-against -eating-cabbage-during-Covid-19-pandemic

Wiborg, J. F., Knoop, H., Stulemeijer, M., Prins, J. B., & Bleijenberg, G. (2010). How does cognitive behavior therapy reduce fatigue in patients with chronic fatigue syndrome? The role of physical activity. *Psychological Medicine, 40,* 1281–1287. https://doi.org/10.1017/S0033291709992212

Wilson, J. (2018, May 19). New documents suggest Las Vegas shooter was conspiracy theorist ——what we know. *The Guardian.* https://www.theguardian.com /us-news/2018/may/19/stephen-paddock-las-vegas-shooter-conspiracy-theories -documents-explained

Wong, E. (2016, November 18). Trump has called climate change a Chinese hoax. Beijing says it is anything but. *The New York Times.* https://www.nytimes.com /2016/11/19/world/asia/china-trump-climate-change.html

Wongpakaran, N., Wongpakaran, T., Pinyopornpanish, M., Simcharoen, S., Suradom, C., Varnado, P., & Kuntawong, P. (2020). Development and validation of a six-item Revised UCLA Loneliness Scale (RULS-6) using Rasch analysis. *British Journal of Health Psychology, 25,* 233–256. https://doi.org/10.1111/bjhp.12404

Wood, M. J. (2016). Some dare call it conspiracy: Labeling something as a conspiracy theory does not reduce belief in it. *Political Psychology, 37.* https://doi.org/10.111 /pops.12285

Yglesias, M. (2018, February 22). The Parkland conspiracy theories, explained crisis actors? The deep state? *Vox.* https://www.vox.com/policy-and-politics/2018/2/22 /17036018/parkland-conspiracy-theories

Yousef, O. (2022, May 26). The Uvalde shooting conspiracies show how far-right misinformation is evolving. NPR. https://www.npr.org/2022/05/26/1101479269/ texas-Uvalde-school-shooting-misinformation-conspiracy-far-right

Zak, A. (2016, November 2). Georgia men plotted attack on Alaska aurora research facility to "release souls," detective says. *Anchorage Daily News.* https://www.adn .com/alaska-news/2016/11/01/2-men-arrested-in-georgia-planned-to-attack-alaska -aurora-research-facility-investigators-say/

Zanella, A. (2018, December 27). George H. W. Bush and the new world order. *Odyssey.* https://www.theodysseyonline.com/george-hwbush

Zarefsky, D. (2014). Conspiracy arguments in the Lincoln–Douglas debates. In *Rhetorical Perspectives on Argumentation, Argumentation Library* (Vol. 24, pp. 195–209). doi:10.1007/978-3-319-05485-8_16

Index

About the Authors

Helen Hendy has a PhD in psychology from the University of California, Riverside. She is now professor emeritus of psychology at Penn State Schuylkill, with seventy peer-reviewed research publications focusing on social factors associated with negative health-related outcomes such as obesity, food selectivity, opioid abuse, anger, PTSD, workplace bullying, and violence. Dr. Hendy's education and research have been supported by grants from the National Science Foundation, National Institutes of Mental Health, and Children's Miracle Network, with two Research Excellence Awards from the Society of Behavioral Medicine.

Pamela Black has a PhD in sociology from the University of California, Riverside. She is now professor of criminal justice at Penn State Hazelton and the discipline coordinator for Social Sciences and Education in the University College. Her primary research focus is on the role of deviant behavior as a coping mechanism, particularly in how it relates to the stresses and strains associated with minority group status. She has published articles on this topic in sociological and psychological journals including *Deviant Behavior*, *Addictive Behavior*, and *Men and Masculinities*. Her book, *Minorities and Deviance: Coping Strategies of the Power Poor*, extended Robert Agnew's general strain theory to a variety of deviant behaviors and was published by Lexington in 2018.